RUSSIA AND EUROPE
IN A CHANGING INTERNATIONAL ENVIRONMENT

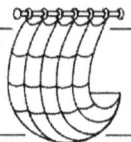

CHAIR INTERBREW-BAILLET LATOUR "EUROPEAN UNION – RUSSIA"

Created in the beginning of the year 2000, the main objective of the Chair Interbrew-Baillet Latour is to encourage the multidisciplinary research of the relations between the European Union and Russia. The Chair Interbrew – Baillet Latour is based on a co-operation between the Instituut voor Internationaal en Europees Beleid of the Katholieke Universiteit Leuven and the Institut d'Études européennes of the Université catholique de Louvain. The research will primarily focus upon an analysis of the origins, determinants and possible evolutions of Euro-Russian relations. Research will be conducted in different fields of study in order to appeal to as well as interest a large public. The academic world as well as political actors and policymakers will find in the seminars, publications and conferences organised by the Chair Interbrew Baillet-Latour the occasion to share their knowledge on Euro-Russian relations, mostly from the viewpoint of International Relations and History.

Parallel to organising these activities on a regular basis, the Chair conducts constant research at each Institute; in this manner a point of interest will be settled at the university and research to the subject of the Chair will be encouraged. Therefore, a Prize of the Chair Interbrew – Baillet Latour has been established at each university to reward the best graduate thesis about euro-russian relations. Emphasising the co-operation between the two universities, the Chair essentially works in French and Dutch ; English and Russian are also used according to the circumstances.

http://www.kuleuven.ac.be/facdep/social/pol/iieb/ibl/Home_BailletLatour.htm

INTERBREW – BAILLET LATOUR FOUNDATION

Presided by Baron Philippe de Schoutheete de Tervaerent, the Foundation's objective is "to encourage and reward through prizes, research scholarships and donations, prestations of high human value with a specific artistic or scientific character."

Katlijn Malfliet and Lien Verpoest (eds.)

RUSSIA AND EUROPE
IN A CHANGING INTERNATIONAL ENVIRONMENT

1425

Leuven University Press
2001

Published with the support of "K.U.Leuven Commissie voor Publicaties".

ISBN 90 5867 195 X
D / 2001 / 1869 / 99
NUR 754

Illustration cover: "Wheel of history" detail from *Wasteland. Atlas* by Maxim Kantor (Courtesy Maxim Kantor and Galerie Eva Poll, Berlin)

TABLE OF CONTENTS

PREFACE

As this book went into press, we received the shocking message that an act of mass-terrorism was committed in New York and Washington on September 11, 2001. The geopolitical paradigm soon appeared to have changed overnight. The news spread that Russia, India and China eventually will become US-partners in the war against terrorism. The European Union is worried about European security and about a shift in US foreign policy priorities.

This book is a selection of papers presented during the academic year 2000-2001 at conferences and seminars in the framework of the "Chair Interbrew-Baillet Latour on the relations between Russia and the European Union". Notwithstanding the unavoidable changes in the geopolitical context after this sudden disastrous event, all contributions happen to retain their value as a reflection on the changing relations between the European Union (or in a broader perspective: Europe) and Russia.

One cannot avoid a certain heterogeneity in the contributions that are gathered. Some articles report on fieldwork, as for example the contributions from Margot Light, John Löwenhardt, Jan Kerkhofs and Koen Vanheusden. Other papers can rather be considered as testimonies from insiders or natives. Igumen Ioann Ekonomtsev brings an insider approach to the role of the Orthodox Church and Vladimir Ronin recalls his own experiences with the specificities of the Russian approach towards Europe. Still others gathered ideas and statements, and their texts can by priority be considered as position papers. We refer in that perspective to the contributions of Yuri Borko, Konstantin Khudoley and Dmitry Danilov.

However, all considerations in this book contribute to a deeper insight in the relations between Russia and Europe. Russia being a strategic partner but perhaps not a strategic ally of Europe. Both, Russia and Europe, take on so many faces and interpretations.

This "status quaestionis" is only a small step in our search for more inspired and creative Euro-Russian relations. The next publications will further venture towards policy-orientation.

Prof. Dr. Katlijn Malfliet,
Research Director Central and Eastern Europe
Lien Verpoest, Research Assistant
Institute for International and European Policy
K.U.Leuven

ACKNOWLEDGEMENTS

The publication of this book was made possible by the help of several people. First of all we would like to thank the authors, for kindly submitting their texts in time. We would like to thank Peter Van Nunen from the MnM Rusland Centrum for translating the texts of Vladimir Ronin and Ioann Ekonomtsev from Russian to English. We would also like to thank Bryan K. Leblang for the first revision of the texts. And last but not least we owe a lot of gratitude to Bart Deceuninck and Richard Sundahl for the thorough and patient correction of the texts.

List of Abbreviations

ABM	ABM Treaty: Anti-Ballistic Missile Treaty
CEECs	Central and Eastern European Countries
CE	Council of Europe
CFE	Combined Forces in Europe
CFSP	Common Foreign and Security Policy
CIS	Commonwealth of Independent States
CJTF	Combined Joint Task Forces
CMEA	Council of Mutual Economic Assistance
CS	Common Strategy
EP	European Parliament
ERRF	European Rapid Reaction Forces
ESDI	European Security and Defence Identity
ESDP	European Security and Defence Policy
EU	European Union
EVS	European Values Study
GDP	Gross Domestic Product
GUUAM	Group of 5 CIS-member states aiming at enhanced co-operation within the CIS: Georgia, Ukraine, Uzbekistan, Azerbaidzhan, Moldova
KFOR	Kosovo Force
MFA	Ministry of Foreign Affairs
NATO	North Atlantic Treaty Organisation
NIS	Newly Independent States
NMD	National Missile Defence
PACE	Parliamentary Assembly of the Council of Europe
OSCE	Organisation for Security and Co-operation in Europe
PCA	Partnership and Co-operation Agreement
PHARE	Poland – Hungary: Aid for Economic Reconstruction (Aide à la Reconstruction Economique)
RF	Russian Federation
RUR	Russian Rouble
TACIS	Technical Assistance to the Commonwealth of Independent States
UN	United Nations
USD	United States Dollar
WEU	Western European Union
WTO	World Trade Organisation

THE EUROPEAN UNION'S RUSSIAN FOREIGN POLICY

Margot Light

1. Introduction

The predominant tone in European Union (EU)-Russian relations in recent times is disappointment and impatience on both sides. EU officials and politicians are, explicitly or implicitly, disappointed that progress in implementing EU-Russian agreements has been so slow, and barely conceal their impatience with the tendency of Russians to indulge in special pleading. There is also considerable irritation at the constant reiteration of Russia's great power status. That claim may have been valid in the past, at least in terms of military power and political weight, but it is manifestly specious in terms of the economic criteria that matter today. The war in Chechnya distresses EU politicians, and the fact that Russian officials apparently disregard their concern embarrasses them by suggesting to their electorates that the EU's policy on human rights is selective. Russian politicians and officials, on the other hand, are equally distressed that the EU does not accept Russia's great power status and treats Russia as if it were any small state. They are offended by EU demands that relate to 'domestic' matters and they perceive EU statements – and sanctions – relating to Chechnya as improper and intolerable. They are convinced that the EU does not understand Russia's specific situation and needs.

The EU's policy towards Russia is set out in a number of agreements and documents. The basis of the relationship is the Partnership and Co-operation Agreement (PCA), which was concluded in June 1994 but only ratified in December 1997. Less than the Europe Agreements that were designed to prepare aspirant states for EU membership, the PCA is, nevertheless, far more than an ordinary agreement on political and economic relations. Its aim is to develop closer political links, foster trade and investment, support the reform process in Russia and create the conditions necessary for the establishment of a future free trade area between the EU and Russia.[1] EU aid to Russia is delivered via the Technical Assistance to Russia and the Commonwealth of Independent States (TACIS). Modelled on the PHARE programme which had been set up to assist the East European former socialist countries, TACIS was established in 1991. The main aim of EU aid to Russia is 'to support transition to a market economy and democracy'.[2] The third important document that sets out EU policy is the Common Strategy on Russia, adopted by EU Member States in June 1999. A new instrument of the Common Foreign and Security Policy (CFSP), the Common Strategy commits EU members to co-operate on policy towards Russia and, in particular, to assist in establishing a 'stable, open and pluralistic democracy in Russia'[3].

A great deal of the discussion about EU-Russian relations on both sides centres on the progress – or lack of progress – in implementing these documents. In relation to TACIS in particular, there is a regular litany of complaints on both sides about the effectiveness of programmes, as well as concern about what might be called the direction of aid – in other words, whether the programmes are designed to help Russia or to give assistance to the Western specialists who participate in them. What is rarely considered in these discussions is the context of EU-Russian relations. Everyone knows that context is important but it is not often taken into account.[4] Yet it is the context that affects rate of implementation of agreements and their effectiveness. In this paper, therefore, I want to point to three aspects of context that are particularly important if we wish to understand EU-Russian relations and that may have a profound effect on the future of those relations.

2. Context

Two aspects of the context in which EU-Russian relations take place are very concrete. First, it has become increasingly clear over the past few years that NATO-Russian relations influence Russian foreign policy in general, including Russia's relations with the EU. Second, the EU's relations with the states of Central and Eastern Europe (CEE) are the background against which EU-Russian relations take place. As we will see, EU enlargement to include some of the CEE states is perceived to have direct consequences for Russia but it also has an indirect effect which will not be discussed here, in that the success of the CEE former socialist states in achieving democratic and market transition serves as a standard against which Russian transition tends to be judged. The third aspect of context that will be considered in this paper is far less concrete than NATO-Russian relations or EU relations with the CEE, but it is no less important. It concerns the psychological effects of exclusion and conditionality on EU-Russian relations. Let us consider each of these aspects in turn.

3. NATO-Russian Relations

NATO expansion is the issue that has had the most profound effect on Russian foreign policy. After the disintegration of the Soviet Union in 1991, liberal westernizers predominated among Russian foreign policy decision-makers. They believed that, since Russia was becoming a democratic state with a market economy, its national interests would be the same as the interests of other democratic capitalist states. They were convinced that NATO would be subsumed within a larger, European-wide, security system. After all, it had been designed as a defence alliance against the Soviet Union and, since the Soviet threat no longer existed, there was no further purpose it could serve. When it turned out that, far from disappearing, NATO intended to enlarge its membership to include some of the former socialist states of CEE, the influence of liberal westernizers on Russian foreign policy was seriously undermined. They were held responsible for NATO expansion – their concessions to the West had made expansion possible. In fact, liberal westernizers did not support NATO's plans to enlarge. Indeed, it is striking that opposition to NATO expansion is virtually universal in Russia: no matter what political views are held on other subjects, NATO is perceived as a relic of the Cold War and NATO expansion is thought to represent a threat to Russia.

The May 1997 Founding Act on Mutual Relations, Co-operation and Security between NATO and the Russian Federation was intended to reassure Russia that it could have a partnership with NATO even if enlargement proceeded[5]. However, while President Yeltsin believed that the Act meant that NATO would have to consult Russia in the Permanent Joint Russia-NATO Council set up by the Founding Act, NATO leaders stressed that Russia would have 'a voice in but not a veto over NATO's business.' Although Russian analysts considered NATO expansion a strategic error, they accepted that Russia could not prevent it occurring and, despite a negative public response to expansion, by the beginning of 1999, it looked as if Russians had accepted the inevitable.[6]

The formal admission of Poland, Hungary and the Czech republic to NATO in March 1999 was followed, however, by the adoption of a new strategic concept at the 50th anniversary NATO Summit in Washington, and the announcement that the door to NATO membership remains open. This caused consternation in Russia – and Kosovo was the final straw. The attack on Serbia confirmed the prejudices of those who were adamantly opposed to good relations with the West and undermined more moderate views. NATO had, in Russian eyes, ceased to be a defence alliance. Moreover, its new strategic doctrine – which stated that NATO would respond with force to threats other than an armed attack on Member States, to 'regional crises', for example, 'at the periphery of the Alliance' – had been seen in action in Serbia and it was perceived to pose a direct threat to Russia[7]. Now that NATO had enlarged, the periphery of the Alliance was also the periphery of the Russian Federation and there was no reason why the new doctrine should not be used to underpin military action in areas that the Russian government considered to be within its own legitimate sphere of influence.

Russians are deeply concerned about further NATO enlargement, particularly since it is highly likely that the next round of expansion will include the

Baltic states. This will bring NATO right up to the Russian border. It is true, of course, that Russia has shared a border with NATO in Norway for many years, but the possible membership of the Baltic states reminds policy makers how vulnerable the USSR was in the 1930s, before the Baltic states were annexed in 1940 and incorporated into the Soviet Union. The concern about the effects on Russia if the Baltic states join NATO is prevalent at all levels of Russian society. In a survey conducted in January 2000, for example, 37 per cent of respondents thought that Baltic membership of NATO would present some or a great threat to Russia, while only 17 per cent saw it as no threat, and 35 per cent did not know[8].

The EU and NATO are, of course, separate organisations and the EU has no jurisdiction over NATO policy. Why then should NATO-Russian relations affect Russia's relations with the EU? One reason is that Russian foreign policy has, in general, become less flexible and co-operative as a result of the tension with NATO. In this sense, NATO is an important part of the context in which EU-Russian relations take place. Ideally, Russians would like the EU to use its influence to prevent a second round of NATO expansion. At the very least, they would like the EU to understand their concern about NATO expansion. As we shall see, however, the connection between NATO and EU policy has recently become even more marked because of EU plans to develop a defence potential.

4. EU – CEE Relations

There is a great contrast between the widespread condemnation of NATO in Russia, and the positive views that are commonly held about the European Union. Few people in Russia perceive any threat to Russia in enlargement, even if the Baltic countries join. EU enlargement was, in effect, perceived as an acceptable alternative to NATO expansion at first. But even after NATO expansion had taken place, so that EU enlargement could no longer be seen as an alternative, approval of the inclusion of new members persisted. As for the general public, a large majority – 74 per cent – believe that it is important that Russia should have good relations with the EU.[9]

Russians may have positive views about the EU in general, but they know very little about it – for example, where its headquarters are, who belongs to it, what it does, or even what kind of relations Russia has with the organisation. There are three reasons for their ignorance. First, international issues have a low profile in Russia. For most of the past decade, events in Russia itself have been so dramatic that they have dominated the news. Second, Russia's relations with the EU are primarily economic and technical; in other words, they concern matters that attract little media coverage in Russia as elsewhere. This explains why the public is not made aware of the EU by the Russian media. The third reason is poor publicity on the part of the EU itself. Given the amount of EU assistance that Russia receives, the European Commission should be disconcerted about the lack of public awareness and it should consider widening the scope of its public relations in Russia.

If few members of the public know anything about the EU, they clearly do not worry about the effects of enlargement on Russia. Officials in the relevant ministries are well aware, however, of the potential hazards of an expanding market that includes the CEE but excludes Russia. Russia's trade relations with CEE countries will, they believe, be adversely affected. Although EU officials assure them that Russian trade will benefit from enlargement, since EU tariffs are lower than those currently levied against Russia by the accession countries, they are not convinced. They are also concerned that more Russian exports might fall victim to EU anti-dumping procedures. Moreover, the EU currently receives 40 per cent of Russia's exports and provides 38 per cent of its imports. As a result of enlargement, Russian exports are likely to exceed 50 per cent, thus increasing Russia's trade dependence on the EU. Russian analysts are also anxious that the asymmetry in Russian-EU trade – one third of Russia's exports to the EU consists of raw materials and minerals, while one third of its imports from the EU comprise consumer goods – will have a negative effect on Russia's future economic development.

Of all the potential negative consequences of CEE membership of the EU, the issue that causes most concern is movement across borders. Once the CEE countries join the Schengen agreement, Russian citizens will require visas to travel to or through them. This is a particularly acute problem for Kaliningrad, which will in due course become a Russian exclave within the EU. Kaliningrad people have to travel approximately 500 kilometers through Lithuania and either Latvia or Belarus in order to get to the rest of Russia. At present they are permitted visa-free transit through Lithuania. After EU enlargement, they will need visas. The EU has, belatedly some might say, recognised the Kaliningrad problem. In a paper prepared by the Commission for the European Council in January 2001, for example, the Commission admits that

"The adoption of the acquis by Poland and Lithuania will inevitably imply changes in some existing rules and practices between Russia, the EU and the new Member States. Some of these changes will have an equal impact on all Russian regions while others will have specific implications for Kaliningrad, mainly on the movement of goods, people, and the supply of energy."[10]

The paper offers no more than 'ideas and options for discussion between the parties'. Yet the problem is urgent given that Poland intends to introduce the Schengen *acquis* in 2001 and Lithuania at the latest upon accession to the EU.

Moreover, the visa issue has practical implications for cross border trade and for divided families well beyond Kaliningrad.

Of course, EU officials and member states are aware that the outsider states (Belarussians, Ukrainians and Moldovans no less than Russians) resent the Schengen restrictions. What they do not comprehend – or what they do not care to accept – is the psychological effect of Schengen, in the sense that it provides concrete confirmation of exclusion from an expanding Europe. In Ukraine, President Kuchma has referred to the new 'paper curtain' of travel restrictions erected by the EU in place of the 'Iron Curtain' dismantled in 1989.[11] There is a bitter irony, to Russians and the people of the other excluded states, in the fact that the demand by the West on the Soviet authorities in the 1970s and 1980s to grant freedom of emigration to Soviet citizens did not translate into freedom of immigration to the West or even free travel rights in Europe and the United States for post-Soviet citizens of the Commonwealth of Independent States.

EU and NATO policy towards Russia has become most inter-related with respect to defence. In June 1999 the European Council agreed to expand the Common Foreign and Security Policy so that the EU would 'have the capacity for autonomous action, backed up by credible military forces, the means to decide to use them, and a readiness to do so, in order to respond to international crises without prejudice to actions by NATO'.[12] The EU aimed to achieve the military capacity to deploy 50 – 60,000 troops by the year 2003 which would be capable of fulfilling the full range of 'Petersberg tasks' (named after the town in which the West European Union, which has been absorbed into the EU, elaborated a list of its tasks): humanitarian and rescue work, crisis management, peace-keeping, and peace-making. At first, Russians welcomed the Common European Security and Defence Policy (ESDP). It might, they believed, offer an alternative European security structure that would diminish NATO's importance in Europe. There was no perception in Russia that the ESDP might represent a threat. On the contrary, the National Security Blueprint adopted in January 2000 which includes an extensive list of 'fundamental threats [to Russian security] in the international sphere' does not mention the European Union. Nor does Russia's new military doctrine adopted in March 2000.[13]

However, discussions within the EU have increasingly emphasised that the ESDP is intended as an addition, not an alternative, to NATO. At the Nice Inter-Governmental Conference in December 2000, for example, the Presidency Conclusions confirmed that 'NATO remains the basis of the collective defence of its members...The development of the ESDP will...lead to a genuine strategic partnership between the EU and NATO in the management of crises'.[14] Although the European Council insisted that Russia, Ukraine and other interested states could be invited to participate in EU-led operations, an ESDP that is an addition to NATO is far less attractive to Russia than an EU defence policy that offered an alternative would be.

The objective is to develop the capacity to conduct EU-led military operations in response to international crises, but only where NATO as a whole is not engaged. If it is to be NATO that decides whether it will respond to a crisis or whether the EU should respond, the ESDP will, in effect, require NATO permission to function. This raises a host of 'sovereignty' issues for the EU itself – in effect, it gives the US, as the undisputed lead decision-maker in NATO, the right to decide when and where EU member states can deploy military force. But it also has serious implications for EU-Russian relations. Russian policy makers can be expected to become less sure about the advantages of the EU developing a defence potential if the ESDP is an adjunct of NATO. Indeed, ESDP as an addition, not an alternative, to NATO signals the possibility of even further isolation for Russia. Moreover, it raises a new dimension of what the consequences of EU enlargement will be for Russia, particularly with regard to former Soviet states becoming EU members. If ESDP is perceived as an adjunct to NATO, Russians will not necessarily retain their positive views about EU enlargement.

5. The Psychological Effects of Exclusion and Conditionality

The third aspect of the context of EU-Russian relations is less tangible than NATO-Russian relations or EU-CEE relations, but it is no less important and it is affected by the other two aspects. In the case of Russia and NATO enlargement, for example, the sense of impotence that resulted from the inability to persuade NATO members that enlargement undermined Russian security contributed to the growing assertiveness in Russian foreign policy that has been evident in recent years. With regard to EU enlargement, it is clear that being left out of a process that is widely believed to be the route to prosperity and well being produces psychological consequences for those who are excluded. But the psychological context of EU-Russian relations is not confined to what might be called the inadvertent and indirect consequences of exclusion from a set of processes taking place elsewhere. There are also psychological effects that emanate directly from the EU's relations with Russia.

The EU's relations with Russia are based on a very explicitly enunciated set of values. As we have seen, the PCA aims to support the reform process in Russia, while EU aid is directed towards supporting Russia's transition to a market economy and democracy and the Common Strategy commits EU members to assisting Russia in establishing a stable, open and pluralistic democracy in Russia. Similar values underpin the EU's relations with the other

CEE states. Indeed, CEE states that wish to accede to the EU are required to have implemented the Copenhagen criteria, two of which are a liberal democratic system of government in which the rule of law and respect for human rights prevail and a market-based economy[15]. In the case of the CEE, however, the reward for adopting these values is membership of the EU with all the benefits that are perceived to result from membership. Whatever the pain to individuals or groups within the CEE that might result from implementing the conditions, the gain that CEE politicians can promise their citizens is the prospect of a standard of living comparable to that of the West European members of the EU. In the case of Russia and the other outsider states, there is no prospect of EU membership in the foreseeable or even distant future. In short, although Russia will be excluded from the process of EU enlargement, EU policy is directed towards assisting Russia in achieving the standards set in the Copenhagen criteria.

Even if EU membership is not a prospect for Russia, the values that the EU stands for are admirable; it is difficult to disagree that Russians would be much better off if those values prevailed in their country. Nevertheless, the attempt to impose a set of values on a country (particularly one that has not been conquered in war) is a relatively new phenomenon in international relations and it has distinct psychological effects on the relationship between the EU and Russia. The didactic, smug and often patronising language of the PCA and the Common Strategy and the conditions attached to TACIS programmes represent a new style of diplomacy and of inter-governmental relations. Gowan refers to an apparent 'tone of condescension and hubris in the EU's approach' to Russia.[16]

It is not surprising that Russians – even those who share the values of the EU and want nothing more than that they should prevail in Russia – find the EU's language objectionable. The most obvious reason why they find it galling is because not so long ago Russia was the largest constituent republic of a superpower and this is not a tone the EU would adopt in its relations with superpowers.[17] The language in which the EU conducts its relations with the EU serves as a constant reminder, therefore, of Russia's diminished status. But there is a more profound reason why Russians resent the EU's tone.

It is often taken for granted in the EU that putting its values into practice will bring about successful economic transition and democratic consolidation. The fact that ten CEE states were deemed by October 1999 to have satisfied the Copenhagen criteria, and therefore ready to begin accession negotiations, is seen to be proof of the proposition. To many millions of Russians, however, it seems evident that the attempt to emulate EU values, to follow EU instructions (which are based on the current orthodoxies of the international financial institutions), and to fulfil EU conditions has caused their impoverishment, their uncertainty about the future, the deterioration not only in their standard of living, but in their chances of staying alive. After all, Russia's gross domestic product declined by 43.3 percent from 1991 to 1998; industrial production fell by 56 percent, and the agricultural decline was even larger. Inflation cut the average real incomes of working Russians by 46 percent in 1992; incomes improved until 1998; but in 1998-99, the population's real disposable income dropped by a third. In absolute terms, the Russian economy is now no larger now than the economies of South Korea or the Netherlands. By 1997, 63 per cent of the population lived below average income levels. Levels of disease and malnutrition are far higher now than in the 1980s and life expectancy (especially for men) has fallen. The population has contracted steadily since 1992 and will continue to decline.[18] In short, economic reform has brought a better life to a very small minority; for the vast majority of Russians, life is a great deal more difficult now than it was a decade ago. No wonder that they, or at least the people who represent them, find the EU's patronising tone unacceptable.

To a large extent these three aspects of the context in which EU-Russian relations take place account for the disappointment and impatience felt by both sides in the relationship and they are likely to go on affecting EU-Russian relations in future.

6. Conclusion

Even though they criticise the normative tone embedded in EU agreements, and resent the intrusiveness of the conditions on which EU assistance depends, most members of the Russian foreign policy elite believe that adopting EU norms would benefit the Russian economy and produce a more stable society. Moreover, as we have seen, public opinion in Russia is, by and large, favourably disposed towards the EU.

EU officials often blame endogenous factors, for example, the lack of a democratic history prior to, and the absence of civil society under communism, for the slow rate of change in Russia. Russians themselves, on the other hand, tend to blame exogenous factors. They find fault, for instance, with the programmes offered by the EU and other international organisations, and with the expectation that one type of reform would fit all the transition states. But it is clear that endogenous and exogenous factors feed into one another in complex ways and contribute to the psychological aspects of the context in which EU-Russian relations take place.

Despite the prevailing sense of disappointment on both sides that EU-Russian relations have not progressed further, conditions are particularly auspicious for an improvement now. Although NATO expansion and the war in former Yugoslavia left most Russians feeling isolated and vulnerable, President Putin seems more determined than his predecessor to bring Russia closer to Europe. Romano Prodi, President of the European Commission, has put forward some interesting initiatives, for example, to integrate Russian energy supplies into Europe and to create a common European economic space. The May 2001 EU-Russia summit reaffirmed that 'EU enlargement should lead to an increase in the volume of economic activity between Russia and the acceding countries, as well as with the enlarged EU as a whole'. It also agreed to make foreign and security policy matters a regular feature of the agendas of the EU-Russia political dialogue meetings at all levels, and decided to establish a joint high-level group within the framework of the PCA to elaborate the concept of a common European economic space.[19]

According to one prominent Russian foreign policy specialist, the EU-Russian relationship needs a new aim which goes beyond simply broadening the activities that are currently included in the EU-Russian agenda: 'not only rapprochement or co-operation but also eventual Russian membership of the EU'. Although it could not realistically happen in less than a generation, 'putting the issue on the agenda would enhance and strengthen Europe's international standing. It would also solidify the western and democratic orientation in Russia'[20]. In short, it might give Russians a goal that would make the pain of further reform more acceptable.

Notes

1   For the text of Russia's PCA agreement, see *Official Journal of the European Communities*, (*OJL*) 327, 28/11/1997.
2   <http//europa.eu.int/comm/external_relations/ceeca/tacis/index.htm>, retrieved 27 May 2001. Apart from the programmes managed by TACIS, EU food aid flows through the European Agricultural Guidance and Guarantee Fund, while humanitarian aid is handled by ECHO. See also Aidan Cox and Jenny Chapman, *European Union External Co-operation Programmes* (London: Overseas Development Institute, 1999).
3   The Common Strategy towards Russia is published in *OJL* (1999/414/CFSP), L157/1, 24 June 1999. The Russian government responded with its own Medium-term Strategy for relations with the EU, published in *Diplomaticheskii vestnik*, No. 11, 1999, pp. 20-28.
4   The study done by the European Commission Forward Studies Unit on five possible scenarios for Europe in 2010 (Gilles Bertrand (Coord.), Anna Michalski and Lucio R. Pench, *Scenarios Europe 2010: Five Possible Futures for Europe*. European Commission, Forward Studies Unit, 1999) does take context into account but it pays little regard to the three aspects considered in this paper.

5   The text of the Founding Act can be found at NATO Handbook, 1998 edition. NATO On-line Library. <www.nato.int/docu/handbook/1998/v070.htm> Retrieved 29 April 2000.

6   An October 1996 poll found that 32 per cent of respondents thought that expansion would harm Russia; by July 1999, 66 per cent believed that it represented a direct threat. Only 14 per cent did not consider it dangerous, while 21 per cent were undecided. See 'Opinion Analysis', Office of Research and Media Reaction, USIA, Washington, D.C., January 24, 1997, M-12-97; Public Opinion Foundation, Moscow. <www.english.fom.ru/reports/frame/eof993003.html>. Retrieved 30 June 2000.

7   The new strategic concept is published in *The Reader's Guide to the NATO Summit in Washington*, 23-25 April 1999 (NATO Office of Information and Press, Brussels, 1999).

8   The nation-wide survey (n=2003) was commissioned from VTsIOM by Stephen White, John Löwenhardt and Margot Light in Russia for their research project *The Outsiders: Russia, Ukraine, Belarus, Moldova and the New Europe*. It is part of the ESRC 'One Europe or Several?' Programme (Project Grant L213252007). Despite the perception that Baltic membership of NATO represented a threat, the respondents did not feel that a NATO attack on Russia was likely. Asked in a separate question about the likelihood of any country attacking Russia in the next five years, 75 per cent thought it improbable.

9   For details of the survey, see n. 8.

10 'The EU and Kaliningrad', Commission of the European Communities, COM(2001) 26, Brussels, 17.1.2001, p. 2.

11 Cited in RFE/RL NEWSLINE Vol. 3, No. 178, Part II, 13 September 1999

12 Cologne European Council, Presidency Conclusions, Press Release: Cologne (04-06-1999) – Nr: 150/99.

13 'Kontseptsiya Natsional'noi Bezopasnosti Rossiiskoi Federatsii' (The Concept of National Security of the Russian Federation), *Nezavisimoye Voennoye Obozreniye*, 14 January 2000; 'Voennaya doktrina Rossiiskoi Federatsii' (The Military Doctrine of the Russian Federation), *Nezavisimaya gazeta*, 22 April 2000.

14 Nice European Council, Presidency Conclusions, ANNEX VI, Nr: 400/1/00, 08-12-2000.

15 The Copenhagen criteria were set to establish eligibility for membership of the EU. See The European Council, Copenhagen, 21-23 June 1993, Conclusions of the Presidency. SN 180/93, p. 13.

16 Gowan D. *How the EU Can Help Russia*. London: Centre for European Reform, 2000, p. 11.

17 The EU would not, for example, make abolition of the death penalty a condition for good relations with the USA; nor did it make critical comments about the flawed process of the last American presidential election.

18 Reddaway P. and Glinski D. *The Tragedy of Russia's Reforms*. Washington, D.C., United States Institute of Peace Press, 2001, p. 3.
19 Joint Statement, EU-Russia Summit, 17 May 2001. <http://europa.eu.int/comm/external_relations/russia/summit17_05_01/statement.htm>. Retrieved 19 May 2001.
20 Sergei Karaganov, *The Financial Times,* 18 May 2001.

Modern Russian Policy Towards Europe

Konstantin Khudoley

1. Russia and Europe: Rapprochement or Estrangement?

During the 18th and 19th centuries, the following tendency could be observed: the further the Russian Empire extended to the West, the more its elite tended to adopt European standards and values, so that Russia was becoming a *European* country. This trend, however, did not appear to be solid enough and was interrupted by the 1917 revolutions. The Soviet Union and – after World War II – the countries of Central and Eastern Europe, where communist regimes were established, found themselves to be isolated from the *other* Europe. New orders and customs running counter to the general direction of European development were forcefully imposed upon these nations. Western expansion of the Soviet Union, in fact, did not contribute to the *European* orientation of Soviet society. The "Iron Curtain" worked very effectively.

The transformations which have marked the last decades of Russian history and have been closely connected with figures such as Mikhail Gorbachev and Boris Yeltsin have lead to dramatic changes. Totalitarian regimes have disappeared; the world socialist system and the Soviet Union have collapsed. Russia has acquired new borders similar to those of the short period of the 1918 Brest Peace Treaty. The surface area of the country has significantly diminished. After centuries of struggle for sea outlets, Russia has finally come to possess only narrow coastal strips. Nevertheless it is possible to state that Russia is closer to Europe today than ever before in the course of its long history.

First, after Finland joined the European Union, Russia obtained an extensive border with the states playing a central role in the integration processes of the continent. This cannot help but influence Russia. The further broadening of the EU will bring a further extension of its common border with Russia and create favourable possibilities not only for co-operation but also for interaction in the field of European integration. Missing these opportunities would be a serious mistake for both parties.

Second, during the 1980s and 1990s, Russia underwent considerable changes in the entire social and political order. Russia has therefore been shaken twice in the course of the 20th century. The first time, a bloody civil war, mass repression, and the death or emigration of millions (comprised of the nation's intellectual elite) accompanied the changes. The second time, the transition has been implemented in a mainly peaceful manner with the exception of some regions. As a result, Russia is moving – though sometimes inconsistently – in the direction of market and democratic reforms. The country has been facing more complications than were originally expected – and more than other states had met. It is obvious now that radical reforms are most fruitful when preceded either by long preparations (as was the case for Poland and Hungary), or where pre-communist traditions have been preserved (Czech Republic and Estonia). Russia had nothing of the above-mentioned. This has resulted in conflicting outcomes: entire segments and structures exist, which reforms have almost bypassed – higher education, judicial system, army, communal spheres, etc. Contrary to expectations, the living standards of most of the population have decreased. Like any revolution, the transitions of the 1980s and 1990s created a number of expectations which were unrealistically high, thus creating even greater disappointment. Unlike the peoples of Central Europe, a significant proportion of the Russians came to refuse not only reformist leaders, but also Western values as a whole. Nevertheless, it would be a mistake to speak of a failure of reforms. One of the most important consequences has been the emergence of a new Russia, which believes in freedom, democracy, and the market. This new Russia is willing to get closer to the West and, in the first place, to Europe. This is in sharp contrast to the old Russia, which still hangs on to remnants of Communist totalitarianism. This new Russian group unites about a quarter of the population, yet it is far from ideal itself, sometimes aspiring to strengthen the economy while ignoring political issues. The polls reveal that a large group of Russians are tending to build their welfare on their own, individualistically, without relying upon the state and without taking part in the election process. Nevertheless, it is these people who are creating the new atmosphere. This group may constitute a minority, but Russia has never before possessed such a significant social base for a policy aimed at integration with Europe.

It would be a mistake, however, to overlook some other regrettable tendencies and phenomena. First of all, Russia and the majority of European countries are at different stages of economic development. If member states of the EU and some others have already entered the post-industrial era, Russia still remains a largely industrial society. The gap in living standards and quality of life not only has not narrowed, but has actually deepened. The border between Russia and Finland is nowadays one of the greatest contrasts, if not the greatest contrast in the world.

Contrary to the majority of former socialist European countries, the Russian elite did not pursue a transatlantic path. Moreover, among a certain segment of this elite there are strong attitudes favouring some special Eurasian path of development for Russia, and there are some who are even looking for inspiration in the experience of the People's Republic of China.

The process of identity formation has still not been completed among the majority of the Russian population. Their values are fluctuating between the European and the Eurasian. This process is fraught with the appearance of new dividing lines between Russia and Europe. However, at the current time the most favourable conditions are present for turning Russian development in the same direction as Europe.

2. Foreign Policy of President Putin: Succession and Changes

"The new political thinking" proclaimed by Mikhail Gorbachev in the second half of the 1980s has put an end to the old dogmas of Cold War stereotypes and confrontation. The Russian leadership kept on course toward partnership with the West in the early 1990s, a time that might be called "the romantic period" in the history of international relations. But it did not last long. Since the mid-1990s, considerable contradictions have been showing up between Russia and the West, which have led to what some are calling the "cold peace" – as opposed to the "cold war". The Kosovo crisis in the spring of 1999 became the lowest point for Russian-Western relations in many years. How can this evolution be explained?

As the reforms began, the Russian political elite believed that Russia would keep its super-power status, just like the US, with the transition being more successful than in the other post-Soviet states, thus establishing Russia as their natural leader. Things did not turn out this way. Russia's position in the world was undermined. This process, predestined as far back as the late Soviet period, when the Soviet Union figuratively was called "the Upper Volta with nukes", was not understood by the elite and many other social groups. This factor started playing a more and more significant role in the determination both of internal and external policy. This state of affairs has been aggravated by the disappointment in Western values experienced by part of the Russian population and the inability of many businessmen (especially those who have become filthy rich on money derived from the state budget) to compete successfully with Western capital.

In its turn, the West revealed a certain inconsistency as well. The complexity of reforms in such a vast country as Russia, deprived of practically any tradition of democratic society and market economy, was not fully realised for a long time. It seems that to some extent this lack of understanding persists even now.

Finally, in the West as well as in Russia, the Cold War inertia turned out to be quite strong. The interest groups whose well being was closely dependent on the Cold War were too numerous and powerful to disappear or even reshape during such a short historical period. Unfortunately, we cannot help but recognise that the second half of the 1990's were filled with attempts to draw public opinion away from internal problems by switching to foreign policy issues. This became most clear during the presidential pre-electoral campaign in 1996, when President Yeltsin attached crucial importance to NATO enlargement (the public opinion interest in the issue was minimal before that), and then in the spring of 1999, when the Kosovo crisis became one of the arguments against impeachment, which is allegedly inadmissible in such a critical international situation.

The foreign policy of President Putin is largely a sequel to the foreign policy of President Yeltsin's second term, though some corrections are apparent. It should be taken into account that Putin's foreign and domestic policies are still in the process of formation, because the power bloc that paved his way to office is characterised by internal contradictions. This cannot but affect an incumbent President's policies, forcing him to postpone some decisions. A certain inconsistency is noticeable in certain doctrines and concepts which were approved in 2000, with some of the different provisions not being adjusted to one another. At the same time Putin is paying great attention to keeping his popularity at a high level, which means making complex and contradictory moves in order to maintain voters' support. It is important to note that Putin has succeeded in this effort. All surveys show that about two-thirds of the voters approve of his activities, and his external policy is meeting with special public acclamation (up to 75 % of all respondents approved of his policy).

Among the specific features of President Putin's foreign policy, we would emphasise the following:

First, Russian authorities understand perfectly well that it is impossible to remain aloof from the globalisation process, and that isolationism will doom Russia to lagging even further behind the leading countries. At the same time there is a widely spread opinion that partial participation is possible in the globalisation process – i.e. partial in the sense of only in the cases where it is profitable for Russia.

Second, the Russian authorities would like to see their country as a major power. At the same time, they realise that this is impossible without the creation of a powerful modern economy and this can be accomplished only by means of further market reforms. In light of this fact, it is no accident that President Putin has appointed advocates of the market economy to leading posts concerned with economic problems in his administration and government. However, along with this, the present Russian administration is focusing to a noticeably greater extent than in the 1990s on military elements of state power.

Third, the present Russian authorities are perceiving the threats of terrorism and separatism with increasing seriousness. Preserving the territorial integrity of the country is one of their main objectives. That is why any direct or indirect support of terrorism or separatism from abroad (or even the expression of sympathy for them) is being regarded as an extremely unfriendly act and is evoking a reciprocal reaction.

Fourth, Russian political leaders understand clearly how important the relationship with the West is. They do not want to break it off and return to the time of the Cold War. A good illustration of this is the fact that already during the 2000 election campaign, Vladimir Putin came out in favour of re-establishing the relationship with NATO and avoided any anti-Western statements although such statements would have given him some additional votes. At the same time, the Russian elite – who believe that the West, and in particular the US and NATO, is paying insufficient attention to the national interests of Russia – are declaring their intention to defend these interests. Certain unreported critical statements in official Russian documents make this point clear. It is very interesting to note that the importance of the idea of a multipolar world, which was a central thesis used to justify the opposition to the US at the end of the 1990's by Boris Yeltsin and Yevgeny Primakov, has gradually disappeared from official Russian documents. Also, it is necessary to mention that the tough tone of some Russian statements is designed for "domestic consumption only" because it reflects the mood of a large part of the electorate.

Fifth, the foreign policy of president Putin is more pragmatic and less ideological. He did not support the regime of Slobodan Milosevic, who had lost the elections. The mediation of Russia in that region contributed to the peaceful change of government. The fact that Russia is reluctant to cancel the debts of some former allies of the USSR, despite the wish to re-establish a dialogue with them, is just one more example of this pragmatic approach.

Sixth, the state support of Russian business in foreign markets and its protection of economic interests was announced by Russian authorities as one of the main aims of its foreign policy. This principle is being put into effect for the export of weapons, though in the future it will be expanded to a wider sphere.

Russia has always attached great importance to the European direction of its foreign policy. Present Russian leaders are paying special attention to it. Official documents relating to the Foreign Policy Concept of the Russian Federation emphasise in the first place that relations with Europe (and equally relations with CIS member states) constitute a priority for Russia. Putin's close contacts with European politicians are not of a fortuitous nature. One definite factor here is the personal sympathy of President Putin for Germany. A number of different events have revealed attempts to influence the US by means of their European allies (British prime minister Tony Blair is the first to be mentioned here).

New accents were also added to President Putin's European policy. First, Russia now assigns the key role in its European policy to the European Union, and not to the OSCE. This can be explained in terms of their more realistic approach to the matter, the European Union being the driving force of integration processes. The somewhat critical attitude towards the OSCE which was caused by the inclusion of the principal proposition regarding humanitarian interventions into the concluding document of the Istanbul summit and by Russian dissatisfaction with OSCE activities in Chechnya should be mentioned here as well.

Second, the Russian attitude towards NATO and its enlargement plans is rather negative. At the same time, Russia wishes to maintain its relations with NATO at a certain level and not to break them off.

Third, the Russian elite is bitterly disappointed about the temporary suspension of the Russian delegation's voting rights at the Parliamentary Assembly of the Council of Europe. This has resulted in a general decline in interest in CE activities.

Fourth, Russian diplomacy is more efficiently combining the simultaneous development of relations with international organisations and their member states. Nowadays when evaluating relations between countries, more attention is being given to the influence of the international organisations they belong to. The Russian government is endeavouring to regulate the regional ties, though it would be wrong to speak of its having ultimate control over them.

Fifth, the Russian government is not demanding any special rights over territories in the former socialist states in Central and Eastern Europe and the Baltic region. It is a significant detail that in official Russian documents the Baltic region is now attributed to Europe and not to the post-Soviet area.

Sixth, Russia is trying to underline its particular role in the CIS more consistently than in the 1990s and is insisting that Europe should consider it when planning its policy.

3. Russia and the European Union

Considerable work was done to develop and strengthen EU-Russian relations during the 1990s. This was the first time that Russia began establishing relations not only with separate member states of the European Union but also with the European Union itself as a supranational organisation.

In 1994 Russia and the EU signed the Partnership and Co-operation Agreement. On the whole this document is rather contradictory. It fixed political relations on a sufficiently high level and created a rather efficient mechanism for co-operation. In the sphere of the economy it has linked a lot of agreements that have been achieved to the accession of Russia into the World Trade Organisation; it has also attempted to use WTO standards in EU-Russian relations even before its accession into this organisation. The 1994 agreement was ratified after a long delay because of the Chechen conflict and certain other events. Many of its provisions have never been implemented because Russia is not a member of the WTO yet.

In 1999, the EU authorities approved the Common Strategy of the European Union towards Russia within the framework of the Common Foreign and Security Policy. It was noted in Russia that this was the first document of its kind to be approved by the European Union. A few months later, the Russian authorities presented their own document on the strategy of Russia towards the European Union. The fact that both partners have initiated a specific dialogue on the strategy of a future relationship is a positive sign. Especially because some concrete provisions that both documents contain are either quite similar or exactly coincide. Of course, it is still early to speak of the complete integrity of strategies. It suffices to mention that one is planned for a 4-year term and the other for 10 years. But the trend toward the development of a strategic partnership is obvious.

It is clear that neither of the parties consider Russia's full or associated membership in the European Union to be possible in the near future. But at the same time many Russian officials are emphasising their desire to continue further advances toward the European Union. The European Union is undergoing important changes. How can these changes affect relations with Russia?

First of all, there are the issues concerning the enlargement of the European Union. Until the summer of 1999 Russia was emphasising that it had no objections against EU expansion. Recently the situation has changed a bit. Russia has declared that it does not object to EU enlargement but it does insist that its interests should be taken into account. In fact, EU enlargement is a rather difficult issue for Russia. To begin with, after the EU accession of Poland and the Baltic States, the Russian external region of Kaliningrad will come to lie completely within the European Union. Both parties agree that Kaliningrad should become a laboratory of co-operation rather than a focus of discord. However it is very difficult to say how to implement this practically. It is often said that Russia and the EU should treat Kaliningrad as a special case. But they differ in their approaches to the issue. Moreover, the Russian constitution does not recognise that regions have any special rights, and the incumbent president wants to equalise the rights accorded to all parts of the federation. This is why it is hardly possible under the present constitution to give Kaliningrad a special status. Thus, the statement of the foreign minister, Igor Ivanov, that the juridical form is not necessary for co-operation in this sphere seems to relate mainly to constitutional issues. It should also be noted that when discussing the Kaliningrad issue, the European Union focuses mainly on the military aspects and environmental problems, while Russia is more concerned about transit and visas. To my mind, the significance of the problem does not allow them to be treated separately.

At the current time it is difficult to say how EU enlargement will affect trade between Russia and Europe. Apart from oil and gas, trade between Russia and the former socialist states in Eastern and Central Europe is minimal. The need for Russian energy resources will remain urgent in Western and Eastern Europe for a long time. But the perspective for other goods is still questionable. In particular, the situation with anti-dumping procedures remains vague. Russia insists that the EU is using anti-dumping legislation most frequently against it (fifteen times already). The European Union claims, in turn, that Russia is committing even more violations, which it prefers to overlook for political reasons.

The Agreement of 1994 proclaimed the objective of establishing a free trade area, i.e. the establishment of free trade in goods and services without any customs or quantitative limitations between the European Union and Russia. Such an undertaking is scarcely possible in the near future. Though no immediate connection was established in the Agreement of 1994 between Russia's joining the WTO and the creation of a free trade area, the European Union is in practice following this principle. This makes the Russian situation quite complicated. In 2000, Russia, Belarus, Kazakhstan and Kyrgizstan created a Eurasian Economic Community. One of these countries – Kyrgizstan – has already become a WTO member. Russia, Belarus and Kazakhstan have applied for membership. It would be advantageous for Russia to join the WTO before Belarus and Kazakhstan because its entrance after these two other nations would occur under less favourable conditions. Finally – and frankly – there is no unity in the views of Russian politicians and scientists on what Russia's joining the WTO will result in. Whether export profits will surpass losses in other sectors of the economy is not clear yet.

The consequences of the introduction of the single European currency, the EURO, are hard to forecast as well. Its gradual replacement of the US dollar in Russian-European trade, especially in the sphere of gas and oil, is still questionable. However certain changes are most likely to happen.

Russia is greatly interested in whether Europe will form military units or not, and if they do decide to do so, in what way. Some politicians and experts hope that Russia will not become a part of NATO, but that it will be able to have a certain level of co-operation in the sphere of military technologies. Others view this process with a certain anxiety, regardless of whether it will be concerned with NATO or not.

In 1997, Finland launched "the Northern Dimension of the European Union" initiative, which it has supported and promoted actively from the time of its EU presidency (second half of 1999) up to the present. Russia appreciates this idea because it is only in the north-west where it will have a common border with the European Union in the foreseeable future. Certain developments have taken place recently, but the initiative is also being restrained by a number of factors. None of the major EU countries have referred to the Northern Dimension as their priority. The Southern countries of the EU take a negative view of the redistribution of European Union funds, and organisational expenditures have not yet been determined. Russia does not have a unified approach either, and the positions of the different north-west regions do not always coincide with one other. They are anxious about the exploitation of natural resources, (an anxiety which is partially justified, because of the extraordinary stress being put on co-operation in this sphere, but the inertia is too strong). There is also an insistence on high technologies being developed more intensively, (though nobody has forecasted the social consequences of such a development yet). Finally, there is a feeling in Russia that the centre of business activity is shifting to the Southern coast of the Baltic sea and it will not be Russia that will benefit most from the Northern Dimension, but rather the EU applicants. This is only a short list of present day problems between Russia and the EU. However, despite the difficulties, a certain amount of positive potential has already been created.

4. Russia and the North Atlantic Treaty Organisation

Relations with NATO were, and remain, one of the most difficult problems of Russian foreign policy. In 1997, top Russian and NATO authorities signed the Founding Act. Both sides affirmed that they do not regard each other as adversaries and that they intend to improve their relations. In Russia many people have a negative view of the Founding Act. From time to time, demands to abrogate this agreement appear among Communist and nationalist-oriented segments of society. It is hard to agree with such an attitude. The existing document has already played – and will continue to play – a positive role in the stabilisation of relations between Russia and NATO. But, of course, it has some weak points. First of all it is not an international agreement and the fulfilment of its provisions depends on the goodwill of its parties. Such an approach is suitable when relations are already established and are developing successfully, but it is dangerous in an initial stage when so many issues depend on the conjuncture of any number of factors, including the internal political struggle. Mutual suspicions did not disappear after the treaty had been signed, because the measures provided for in the Founding Act were insufficient to achieve this end. Some wordings of the document were interpreted differently almost from the very beginning. On the whole it was a compromise, which did not exclude divergent directions of development in the future. And that is the direction developments in fact took.

In 1999 the most serious crisis in the last 10-15 years arose between Russia and NATO. Events in Kosovo were the reason that relations nearly broke down. Fortunately, they began to recover as a result of the KFOR co-operative work that was started in the summer of 1999. Since February 2000, relations between NATO and Russia have gradually been improving. At the present time they are at the same level as before the Kosovo crisis in the spring of 1999. Nevertheless a variety of possibilities still exist for the further development of NATO-Russia relations. Both parties will try to avoid extreme solutions, which could possibly lead to a new rupture of relations. Variants will therefore be sought among those solutions which can enable the preservation of relations.

President Putin has mentioned several times the idea of Russia possibly joining NATO. Some people in Russia and in the West suppose it to be a pure propaganda move and compare it to the USSR's demarche in 1954. The situation is more complicated, however. It would never have been possible for the Soviet Union to join NATO since it did not share the basic values of the NATO member states. The same cannot be asserted categorically in the case of Russia, however, since – despite all obstacles, problems, and sometimes even retrograde developments – Russia is evolving in the direction of a Euro-Atlantic community. In the long-term perspective, well-directed mutual efforts could result in such an approach. So the idea cannot ultimately be put aside, though its practical implementation will become possible only in the distant future.

A co-operation agreement between NATO and Russia without Russia's official joining of the Alliance seems to be a more realistic possibility. Under modern conditions it would offer the optimal framework for co-operation. However, the present situation is not favourable even for that kind of agreement. Therefore, the development of relations on the basis of the Founding Act seems to be most probable.

The restriction of the arms race is a top-priority question, which will undoubtedly play a very important role in the Russia-NATO relationship. The idea of building the national anti-missile defence system has won significant support in the US. The deployment of the NMD requires much preparatory work and the system would not be ready for some years. But the US withdrawal from the 1972 ABM Treaty could seriously destabilise the situation. There is special concern for efforts to ensure the non-proliferation of nuclear and other types of weapons of mass destruction, which are losing their relevance because of the current situation on the international scene. The Russian authorities are endeavouring to offer alternatives that will guarantee missile security in Europe.

Unfortunately, Europe has become the arena of several bloody conflicts in recent years, in particular on the territory of the former Yugoslavia. Immediately after Bosnia and Kosovo, Macedonia became involved in the conflict. Since state and ethnic boundaries in the Balkans do not coincide, and because international and religious conflicts have deep historical roots, the situation in the Balkans will remain tense for a long time. Successful peacekeeping is hardly possible without the participation of both NATO and Russia, working together in the process of conflict resolution.

The NATO-Russia relationship will be further aggravated with the expansion of the North Atlantic Treaty Organisation. The NATO accession of Poland, the Czech Republic and Hungary, coupled with the Kosovo bombings, produced a very painful reaction in Russia. Russia is raising strong objections against a new expansion of NATO, and in particular against the accession of former Soviet republics.

The general negative perception of NATO in Russian public opinion is based on a different motivation. Certain segments of the Russian population are afraid of the revival of military confrontation and the appearance of a new Berlin Wall to the East of the old one. Others are critical of the methods by means of which the Alliance enlargement is being implemented. The most negative criticism can be formulated this way: after NATO and EU enlargements in the Baltic and Central and Eastern European states, Russia will be the only large state left outside these highly influential organisations and its role in European politics will be drastically diminished. If we do not want new dividing lines to appear in Europe, we cannot ignore this aspect of the problem.

5. Russia and the Council of Europe

Russia became a member of the Council of Europe in 1996. The insistence of the first president of Russia, Yeltsin, played a key role in this event because it was the central focus of his policy aims. His indisputable achievement is that he did everything in his power to include Russia in the European system of protection of human rights and freedoms. The values espoused by the Council of Europe were taken into account in the constitution of 1993.

At the same time the activity of Russia in the Council of Europe faces difficulties and problems. First of all, there is Chechnya. The first Chechen war was one of the reasons why the Council of Europe postponed the accession of Russia. The second Chechen conflict, which continues to the present day, became a reason for even tougher criticism. The criticism ultimately led to the suspension of the voting rights of the Russian delegation. The situation in Chechnya is still rather complicated and cannot be evaluated in any simple manner. After the collapse of the USSR in 1991, Chechnya revealed itself to be a traditional society in which Islamic Shari'ah rules and where kidnapping provides one of the most profitable business opportunities. After an agreement in Khasa'vyurt (1996), Russia for all practical purposes left Chechnya, but the Chechen authorities showed an inability to create their own state system. The situation in Chechnya has spun out of control. The aggression of Chechen extremists against Daghestan in the summer of 1999 resulted in the resuming of military operations. Protection of the rights of civilians under such conditions of a military operation is an extremely difficult task. This task is particularly complicated in Chechnya because of the tremendous differences between the various local ethnic populations. Russian troops sometimes violated human rights, as well. It suffices to mention leaflets spread in the fall of 1999, in which the Russian Command declared that everyone who stayed in Grozny after a given period provided for escape, would be treated as a bandit. Later these statements were disavowed.

It would be a mistake to overlook the fact that while implementing its policies in Chechnya, Russia has been taking into account the position of public opinion in Europe and particularly that of the Council of Europe. The Council of Europe Commissioner for Human Rights, Alvaro Gil-Robles, visited Chechnya and had an opportunity to observe the situation closely. There are some foreign assistants accepted on the recommendation of the Council of Europe among the staff members of the Commissioner for Human Rights of the President of Russia. This institute contributed to the restoration of a judicial system in Chechnya. Several Russian servicemen accused of war crimes, as well as Chechen terrorists, are under legal proceedings. But these legal proceedings face serious obstacles, not in the least because of the split in Russian public opinion on how to judge their actions.

Recently, the Council of Europe has been concerned to some extent with the issue of mass media freedom in a number of countries, Russia included.

A much more complex and serious problem is the fact that Russia has not harmonised its judicial system in accordance with the obligations it took upon itself as a member state of the Council of Europe. All the main provisions were set down in the Constitution of 1993, but the concluding section (which describes the procedure for putting the constitution into force) provides that articles dealing with the judicial system, criminal code and certain other reform laws enter into force only at the end of a transition period. The exact length of the transition period was not fixed and all attempts made to remedy the situation have so far failed.

President Putin undertook the latest such effort when he introduced a bill to this end in the Duma, (which soon had to be recalled). Formal objections concerned financial matters: the annual budget had already been adopted and no additional funds had been reserved for undertaking a judicial reform and creating several thousand offices for new judges. But the most probable reason was the opposition of the General Prosecutor's Office (because of the transfer of authority in favour of the Law Court), the Ministry of the Interior and some other bodies. Lately, the Deputy Head of the President's Administration, Dmitry Kosak, stated that the bill would soon be introduced anew in the State Duma.

Russian citizens aspire to enjoy the rights provided by Russia's membership in the Council of Europe. Some of them have already appealed to the European Court for Human Rights in Strasbourg. Some cases are currently being considered. The cases mainly concern violations of social rights (pensions, payment of wages, etc.). The Russian government tends to settle these conflicts before their examination by the European Court. Yet it is unclear whether this policy will be effective. On the whole, and despite a number of problems, Russia's joining the Council of Europe has fostered the growth of human rights and democratic freedom within the Russian legal system.

6. Russia and the Organisation on Security and Co-operation in Europe (OSCE)

Russia's European policy has been centred on this organisation for a long time. It should be admitted that the process of multilateral negotiations initiated by the Helsinki Council on Security and Co-operation was of great significance. It is necessary to emphasise that it played an important role in the peaceful transition from totalitarianism to democracy for most Eastern European countries. Nevertheless, in the 1990s the influence of the OSCE began to decline. Among the different reasons, the following should be stressed. Recently, a number of countries were included in the OSCE, an organisation which appeared in the post-Soviet area. Among them were also Asian states that did not share many European values. Countries such as Tajikistan and Bosnia, whose vital capacity is often considered to be doubtful, became members of the OSCE. Finally, the OSCE mechanism formed during the Cold War period when agreements (often non-formal understandings) played a crucial role in world politics. For the current situation it is an unsuitable co-ordinating mechanism that has become much more complicated.

In the middle of the 90s, Russia proposed to transform the OSCE into a UN type of organisation for Europe, with its own Executive Committee acting similarly to the UN Security Council. But this idea has not gained acceptance. Currently, the majority of OSCE member states are more likely to strengthen their ties with the more wealthy and influential European Union and NATO than to consolidate – investing additional funds – around the OSCE. This is the reason why OSCE activities have been losing their all-embracing character and are becoming more and more fragmentary.

One of the most painful issues is the CFE Treaty. Its operability was paralysed for some time because absolute limits were set for military alliances and not for separate states. At the Istanbul summit in 1999 the treaty was adjusted for the new conditions, with many Russian proposals being taken into account. At the same time, Russia launched an initiative for arms reduction in its north-western region. As for the south of Russia, there are certain problems not only in connection with Chechnya (which are predicted to settle down in the near future because of the withdrawal of regular troops), but also with the Russian military presence in Georgia (peace-keeping forces in the conflict zone in Abkhasia). The instability in the Caucasus which is threatening the south of Russia is an issue which cannot be ignored.

Certain achievements of OSCE activities aimed at the protection of national minorities' rights should be mentioned. Russia takes a positive view of the participation of the OSCE and the Council of Europe in securing the rights of the Russian-speaking population in the Baltic. The European organisations have undoubtedly played a pivotal role in a general trend to improve this situation. The role of the OSCE in conflict settlement is less noticeable nowadays, but it can hardly be ignored.

THE RUSSIAN PERCEPTION OF EUROPE

Yuri Borko

The answers we get depend on the questions we ask. Even the same question can be put in a different wording and different answers will follow. One Russian institute specialised in public opinion polls asked its respondents whether the West intends to disband Russia. 76% of the respondents answered "Yes", as opposed to 24% who answered "No".[1] Another centre for public opinion studies asked the following question: "What type of state do you see as being appropriate for Russia in the future?" Several answers were at the respondent's disposal. A Western type of state was preferred by 43%, the socialist state (as conceived by the USSR) by 22%, and a unique model of the state in accordance with the unique pattern of Russia's development by 16%.[2] Both polls were carried out in 1998. It seems that there is no possible way to come to any conclusion regarding the Russian perception of the West based on these data.

When it comes to analysis and conclusions, one must be very cautious. This relates not only to these or some other data interpreted by Russian researchers and journalists, but also to the Western mass media that supply the population with information on Russia. Unfortunately, a substantial part of it is misinformation.

A detailed analysis of the topic under consideration can be based on two theses:

1. The Russian perceptions of Europe have always been of a contradictory character. This is almost a tradition. These perceptions and feelings are a mixture of attraction and repulsion, acknowledgement and negation, delight and dislike. Russia seems to strive both to adopt the European knowledge and experience, and to repudiate it in the name of the Russian uniqueness. Russians want both to open a "window on Europe" and, at the same time, to board it up. As a rule, the tension in this twofold attitude tends to become aggravated at crossroads in Russian history. This is exactly the case at the present time.

2. Despite the widespread image in Europe of an anti-European Russia, a positive attitude towards Europe in fact prevails in Russia at the current time. Most ordinary citizens, however, remain indifferent to this issue because of everyday preoccupations and troubles. It is exactly this indifference that is a potential source of danger for future relations between Russia and an integrated Europe. But as for now, both parties still have time to prevent negative trends and strengthen their partnership and co-operation.

The above mentioned twofold perception of Europe surfaced in Russia long before the famous discussion between the Russian "westerners" (the *zapadniki*) and the "slavophiles" in the 19th Century. We can recall two prominent Russians from the 17th Century – the clergyman Avvakum, a steadfast "europhobe", and Afanasy Ordin-Nashchekin, a diplomat and the head of Russian diplomacy for some years, who was an ardent advocate of internal reforms in Russia with the European experience in mind. The list of "europhiles" and "europhobes" can be extended.

The point is that the border between these "philes" and "phobes" crossed not only through the upper stratum of the political and intellectual elite, and through Russian society as a whole, but it dichotomised the individual person's opinion, as well. Although this assertion might seem somewhat irrational and fantastic, one could nevertheless compile a list of Russians who personify this contradictory perception of Europe. Alexander Gertsen (Herzen), Fedor Tyutshchev, Mikhail Bakunin and Ivan Turgenev all embody to some extent this persona. The founders of the slavophile's concept have to be included in this list as well. All of them – Konstantin and Ivan Aksakov, Ivan and Piotr (Peter) Kireevsky, Alexander Khomyakov – repeated many times their deep respect for European culture and its important role for Russia. From this point of view, they differ to a great extent from the contemporary Russian quasi-successors of the so-called "Euro-Asianism", who tend to ignore or underestimate this fact of Russian and European history.

Vladimir Ulyanov-Lenin played a crucial role in our history in the 20th Century. At the very beginning of his revolutionary activity, he was inspired with the idea of Russia's transition from Asian barbarism to the European pattern of civilised state and society. He wrote about this in 1894. It is a striking fact that he returned to this idea at the end of his life. In his article "Pages from a Diary", written in January 1923, he emphasised that the country remains in a state of "half-Asian" cultural backwardness and must make "enormous efforts to achieve the level of the common civilised state in Western Europe".[3] It is both a paradox and a tragedy that the man inspired by European ideas and experiences contributed more than anybody else to the building of a state and a society that in principle was incompatible with Europe.

This presentation of prominent people ends with Alexander Blok, a poet of the "Silver Century" of Russian culture. It would be quite difficult to translate his famous verse "Scythians" into English. Instead, a prosaic version can be offered of the most important metaphor regarding the Russian attitude toward Europe. According to Blok's fantasy, Russia is a Sphinx which is looking at Europe with 'hate and love'. This is a hyperbole, a poetical exaggeration that arose from the above-mentioned twofold Russian vision of Europe.

This *"philes-phobes"* polarisation of the Russian attitude toward Europe can be compared to the twofold European perception of Russia. After his travels across Russia, Marquis Astolphe de Custine published the book *"La Russie en 1839"*. Apart from numerous bright and very accurate pictures of Russian everyday life, he was possessed by the idea of a Russian plot against Europe. According to him, Russia looked at Europe as if it were a loot waiting to be seized because of the dissension among Europeans.[4] Some years later, in 1849, another Frenchman, Victor Hugo, took the floor at the Congress of the European pacifist movement in Paris. His famous speech on the United States of Europe was quoted by all the adherents of this idea. It was a surprising fact, but Russia was the second country – after France, but before Italy, Britain, and Germany – named by him as a potential member of this union.[5] Did this famous French writer and democrat know about the despotism, bureaucracy, and serfdom in Russia? This rhetorical question does not need to be answered. If he knew of it, then what were his reasons for including Russia in the list? Did he take into consideration the tangle of historic fates, or the so-called 'Concert of Major European Powers', or perhaps the common Christian values and deep cultural interdependence? We do not know. In any case, Victor Hugo's perception of Russia differed significantly from that held by de Custine.

What are the reasons for this short excursus into the European perception of Russia? Firstly, it confirms my thesis concerning the parallel polarisation of mutual perceptions, both in Russia and in Europe. Secondly, it underlines the fact that in many cases Russians and Europeans used similar or comparable 'pro and con' arguments that were historic, geopolitical, social and cultural in nature. One can almost speak of a 'mirror effect'. This is an interesting question for reflection and discussion. However, a third reason for the excursus is that the opposite perceptions of the 'Other' cannot be analysed in terms of truth and delusion, no matter whether this 'Other' is Russia or Europe. In other words, European polarised perceptions of Russia are nothing but perceptions of different aspects of Russian life (history, society, political regime, culture, etc.), as well as different aspects of European-Russian interaction. The same goes for Russian polar perceptions of Europe. The core of this approach to the endless contest between 'philes' and 'phobes' is a conception of a multi-dimensional and contradictory relationship between Europe and Russia. A list of these 'dimensions', or various sorts of interactions, is long, ranging from climate, natural life, and comparable size to the renowned European dramatist William Shakespeare and the renowned Russian writer Fedor Dostoevsky. Thus, the perception of the 'Other' depends on the criteria chosen. When applied to all the sets of interaction between 'We' and the 'Other', these particular criteria result in a generalised perception of this 'Other'. As a rule, however, this generalisation is incorrect. This relates to the European vision of Russia and vice versa.

The European criteria applied to Russia are beyond the scope of the present analysis. As far as the Russian criteria are concerned, a look through Aleksandr Blok's 'hate and love' bifocal spectacles will help us see Europe from a Russian point of view. The reasons for this 'love' were evident. The first was Russia's striving for modernisation in the 18th and 19th centuries, which meant *de facto* Europeanisation. Further reasons included the admiration of the Russian intelligentsia for the Renaissance and the Enlightenment, together with the closeness of the two cultures to one another based on their common Christian values.

The reasons for the 'hate' were of a more composite origin (once again stressing the fact that this definition is a poetic hyperbole; 'dislike' or 'estrangement' would be more correct terms). We can try to enumerate some of the sources of this feeling which, in and of itself, seems so irrational. One of them is a gap between the 'ideal' and the 'real'. Many Russians were inspired by European ideas and theories, by such mottos as 'Habeas corpus', 'social contract', 'justice', 'liberté, egalité, fraternité', 'democracy', Communist 'Utopia', etc. Many of them were disappointed after their more or less long stay in European countries. Moreover, they felt they had been deceived as they discovered a sharp contrast between the ideals and the realities of everyday life. One can find in their memoirs angry and bitter philippics against hypocrisy, the treachery of ideals, dirty political games, and the gulf between richness and poverty in Europe. Another source of hostility – or at least estrangement – was metaphysical in nature. Bear in mind the different interpretations of certain basic values and social principles, such as for example the concept of freedom, individual versus collectivity, traditionalism versus modernism, human rights and the sources of supreme power. The Orthodox-Catholic contrast should be mentioned as well. It seems that there was, in many cases, a half-latent inferiority complex underlying this negative perception of Europe. This complex resulted from failed or unfinished reforms in Russia and from the failure of the very concept of development to achieve the level of the most advanced European countries.

The last attempt at a 'breakthrough' occurred in the second half of the 19th century and the beginning of the 20th century. Gregory Fedotov, a Russian theologian and philosopher of the first half of the 20th Century, wrote that the period of Russian history from Peter the Great until the First World War was an epoch of triumph of Western civilisation in the Russian Empire. According to Fedotov, during a 50 year period Russia moved from halfway to full Europeanisation. The country needed another 50 years, but was deprived of that opportunity in 1917, when Russian Bolsheviks headed by Lenin captured power.[6] It is a paradox of history that the rulers of the Soviet Union, while being inspired by the European ideas of socialism and communism, built a truly anti-European society.

The question is whether Russia is closer to Europe now in comparison with the beginning of the 20th Century, or whether the gap has in fact become even wider. This is not a simple question. At first sight, the distance seems even wider. There are several arguments of an economic, political, and social nature in favour of this thesis. However, at present, Russia is an industrialised and urbanised society with a high level of education, a great cultural potential (in spite of enormous losses), and unprecedented possibilities for acquiring information and knowledge of all the countries and events of the world. In fact, most of the urban population has accepted Western standards of life. This relates not only to consumption, but also to certain other values such as free choice of enterprise and occupation, free movement of people, free information, and the importance of professional skill and education. Russia is a modernised country now, although it remains overburdened with stereotypes and prejudices inherited from the Soviet past.

These new features of contemporary Russia, as compared with the beginning of the 20th Century, have contributed to the evolution of Russian perceptions of Europe and the West as a whole. At the turning points in our history, the polarisation of attitudes toward Europe have tended to increase. This is the case now, as well. Some data confirm this trend. However, they do not confirm the revived stereotype of an "anti-western" and "anti-European" Russia. The analysis made by Dr. Pavel Kandel, senior researcher at the Institute of Europe in Moscow, confirms this theory. In his article *"The West and Russia as they are viewed by Russian public opinion"*, he writes that "Judgements of Russian citizens with regard to Europe and the United States, as well as with regard to Russia's relations with its Western partners, not only do not remain within the imposed concepts, but quite often are more rational than the new theoretical interpretations of them".[7] Dr. Kandel comes to the conclusion that now is a proper time to pay attention both to the prejudices of mass consciousness and to the delusions of the schemes of political scientists and sociologists.

As already mentioned, the answers we get depend on the questions we ask. We can distinguish between two kinds of questions. One type appeals to ideological or even mythological stereotypes, whereas the other type is aimed at obtaining real perceptions of Europe based on information, priorities and – last but not least – common sense. When respondents to a poll were asked to choose between two statements: "Russia should live according to the same rules as the Western countries", or the contrary, "Russia is a peculiar country alien to the West", 71% of them chose the second point of view.[8] The ideological character of the question was evident, and the possible answers were limited and biased.

Russian perceptions of Europe are analysed on the basis of the responses to two questions:
– Where is Russia now?
– What is the preferable pattern of Russia's relations with Europe and the West as a whole?

As far as the first question is concerned, respondents were asked to define the place of Russia in the contemporary world from three points of view: that of the national economy, that of the national culture, and that of the national character. Three different answers were proposed: closer to Europe, closer to Asia, and in between. The distribution of answers was as follows:
1. The Russian national economy is closer to Europe – 22.8%, closer to Asia – 51.3%, in between – 25.9%.
2. The Russian national character is closer to Europe – 44.3%, closer to Asia – 16.6%, in between – 39.1%.
3. The Russian national culture is closer to Europe – 59.8%, closer to Asia – 16.8%, in between – 23.6%.[9]

The distribution of the answers on the first question differs sharply from that of the rest of the answers. Most respondents considered the Russian economy to be underdeveloped. A pro-European perception of the Russian character and culture prevails over a pro-Asian one. This relates to the national culture in particular (about 60%), whereas a large portion of the respondents (about 40%) were not able to define the place of the national character. The main problem for them was the very concept of the Russian 'national character'. The concept of 'national culture', on the contrary, proved to be more comprehensible for respondents.

These results correspond with another poll carried out by the "Public Opinion" Foundation in January 1999. Being asked to define the place of Russia, 45% of respondents answered that, according to its history, traditions and culture, Russia is closer to Europe, whereas 16% of them view the country as being closer to Asia, and 38% of respondents found it difficult to give a definite answer.[10]

Two polls relate to preferable political and economic systems. In a poll carried out in October 1998, the respondents were asked what national political system would be appropriate for Russia. 25.4% of them named the US (presidential republic), 14% – France (a balanced distribution of power between president and parliament), 9.7% – Germany (parliamentarian republic), 3.7% – the United Kingdom (constitutional monarchy). All of the above comprised a total of 52.8% of the respondents, as opposed to 19.5% of the respondents who chose for the Soviet system. As far as the economic system is concerned, Russia's transition to the market economy was viewed as a progressive process, in full or partially, by 46.3% of the respondents, whereas 39% of them considered it a 'great mistake' or even the 'deliberate destruction of Russia'. The source of this split is evident: namely the very contradictory and painful character of this transition process in Russia. Nevertheless, 64.4% of respondents are in favour of a mixed economic system (market economy controlled and regulated by the state), as compared with 13.7% in favour of a centralised and planned economy (socialist economy) and 8.7% for the free market system.[11]

It seems apparent that most Russians feel sympathy for Europe. Nevertheless, we get a different picture from the final item, which enquires about the Russian perception of the advisability of having closer relations with the west, and with European countries in particular. In fact, the idea of an alliance between Russia and the West is less popular in Russia now than in the early nineties. This negative trend has resulted from several factors, including the worsened economic and social situation in Russia and certain recent actions of the West, such as NATO expansion and its actions against Yugoslavia in particular. Nevertheless, co-operation with the West remains the most appropriate scenario for Russians.

The analysis of short-term fluctuations of these relations resulting from certain current events is a difficult undertaking. Only one case will be examined here. In March 1999, 33% of the respondents expected a revival of the 'Cold War' climate in Russia-NATO relations, whereas 41% of them thought that these relations would gradually return to 'normal'. Five months later, in August, the first point of view was chosen by 17% and the second one by 53%. This poll was carried out by the Russian Centre for Public Opinion Studies. Another poll carried out by the same Centre was intended to determine the general attitude of Russians toward relations with the West. The respondents were asked whether Russia should strengthen mutually beneficial links with the Western countries or whether it would be better to be independent from them. The results were as follows: September 1998 – 46% for the first scenario as against 41% for the second one, May 1999 (peak of Kosovo crisis) – 35% as against 52%, January 2000 – 68% as against 19%.[12] An amazing result! However, when asked whether Russia and the Western countries are ready to co-operate, the respondents proved to be cautious. 38.3% of them answered that both the parties are ready, 13.5 % that only the West is ready, 9.9% that only Russia is ready, and 18.3% that neither party is ready. The aggregated share of sceptics is greater than that of optimists.

Reference to the results of a poll carried out by the Institute of Sociological Analysis (Moscow) in February 2000 will be helpful in completing the analysis.[13] They relate to preferences of the electorate at the time of the presidential elections in March 2000.

Table 1 (% of respondents)

Model of State	Model you prefer	Expected model of Putin
Monarchic empire (Russia until 1917)	4	3
USSR state pattern	22	6
Western state pattern	39	38
Unique state pattern	28	25
It's difficult to define	8	29

Three conclusions can be derived from this table. Firstly, the share of adherents of the Western pattern of the state is at the top. Secondly, most of them expect that Vladimir Putin is going to choose the Western model, whereas most adherents of the Soviet pattern do not believe that the new President will accept their preference. Thirdly, the share of expectations in favour of the Western pattern is larger than the sum of the rest of the expectations. However, supporters of the Western type of state do not form a majority in both columns. Russian society has not made its choice yet.

Table 2 (% of respondents)

Pattern of regime	Regime you are in favour of	Expected model of Putin
Western liberal-democratic regime	51	45
Pinochet's regime of the "hard hand"	11	17
One party regime, like in China	4	4
One party regime, like in USSR	18	5
It's difficult to answer	16	29

This table shows that the share of people who are in favour of a system based on the market economy, the rule of law, and the priority of human rights is largest, and that they are in favour of the Western pattern of the state. In fact, a transition to the market system is now supported by the majority of Russians. Some other recent polls confirm this conclusion. However, this majority is insignificant and unstable, which means that the coming two or three years will be of crucial importance.

Table 3 (% of respondents inclined to vote for Putin)

Regime which you are in favour of					
	Western	Pinochet's	Chinese	Soviet	Unsure
People for Putin	63	12	4	11	11

Hence, two-thirds of the respondents who were going to vote for Vladimir Putin linked their preference with the expectation of his future choice in favour of the Western pattern of state and society.

The analysis of these data can be summarised as follows:

– On the whole, the pro-western preferences of Russian society are currently manifesting themselves more strongly among society as a whole than among the political and intellectual elite.

– Moreover, if Putin implements the above-mentioned course for strategic partnership with the European Union, it will be supported by half of the population and opposed by about 30%. In other words, the political pre-conditions for implementing this course are more favourable than at any time in the nineties, except perhaps for a very short period of general euphoria immediately after the fall of Communism in the USSR.

– The trend reflected in these conclusions is being reinforced by favourable economic factors, i.e. a new period of stabilisation after the financial crisis in August 1998.

Notes

1 A poll carried out by the programme "Observer", TV-6, 15/11/1998.

2 Kandel P. 'The West and Russia as they are seen by the Russian public opinion'. – *Sovremennaya Evropa* No 2, (Moscow: Contemporary Europe, 2000) 30.

3 Lenin V.I. *Works* 4th ed., Vol.33, p. 423.

4 de Custine A. *La Russie en 1839.* Bruxelles, 1843.

5 Victor Hugo, *Oeuvres.* Paris, 1885.

6 Fedotov G. "Russia and Freedom" In: *Thinkers of the Russian Diaspora: Berdyaev, Fedotov* Saint Petersburg, Science, 1992. 420, 436-437.

7 Kandel P. *Op. cit.* p. 28.

8 *The population of Russia under crisis: frames of mind, estimates, prognoses.* Moscow, 1998, 231 (in Russian).

9 Kandel P. *Op.cit.* p. 79.

10 Kandel P. *Op.cit.* p. 30.

11 *The population of Russia under crisis: frames of mind, estimates, prognoses.* Moscow, 1998, p. 224-229.

12 Kandel P. *Op. cit.* p. 34.

13 Kutkovets T., Kliamkin I. 'What does Russia expect from Putin?' – *Moscow News* No 9, 7-13 March 2000, p.8-9.

VALUES IN RUSSIA: AN INTRODUCTION

Jan Kerkhofs

1. Introduction

On the first page of his *"Russia and the Idea of the West"*, Robert D. English quotes from James Joll: "It is only by studying the minds of men that we shall understand the causes of anything".[1] In 1981, the European Values Study Foundation launched its first survey on values, which was restricted solely to the West.[2] The survey was repeated in 1990, based on national samples of 1000 to 4000 interviews of about one hour each, this time covering also Central Europe and a part of Russia.[3] The third wave, in 1999-2000, covered the whole of Western, Central and Eastern Europe (as well as the US), thus becoming representative of about 900 million people. This means that the results for Russia, Ukraine and Belarus are now at our disposal. Of course, such a vast enterprise cannot dig very deeply into the minds of people. Dostoyevsky, Tolstoy, Chekhov, Solzhenitsyn, Chaikovsky, Tarkovsky, etc. are often much more subtle eye-openers in scrutinising the secrets of the Russian soul. It is our hope that this contribution may nonetheless provide some insight into the mentality of our great neighbours to the East.[4]

In order to create an understanding of Russia, the Russian results will be compared with those of Ukraine and of Flanders (sometimes of Belgium as a whole), as well as with another small country, the Republic of Ireland (a country with values that are often closer to those of the US than those of Europe). The reason is simple: specific identities are better understood when compared with other specific identities. Moreover, the survey shows that, generally speaking, Flanders and Belgium are symptomatic for the average Western European. A few preliminary remarks are crucial to further understanding. To study changes in mentalities, one needs successive surveys. These exist only partially for Russia and not at all for Ukraine. This means that the survey is limited to the comparison of age groups. Concerning Belgium and most Western European countries, a certain break is noticeable in the opinions and attitudes between, on the one hand, the great-grand-parents and the grand-parents, and, on the other the parents and the children. Moreover, the younger generations have enjoyed a longer period of education, particularly of higher education. This latter factor is true in the West, as well as in Russia. As a consequence, younger people tend to be more critical and less attached to traditions. This trend seems somewhat more characteristic in the West than in Russia. Finally, to understand what is going on in the minds of the people, historical factors are of the utmost importance. Thus, even after the Enlightenment and the rather recent secularisation process, Europe still remains divided into Roman Catholic, Protestant and Orthodox parts.

2. Background

The degree of importance that the interviewees attach to six basic domains of life provides a general framework to start with. One can begin with a look at Europe in general and then at the four countries. It is striking that everywhere the order of these domains is about the same (comparing, as far as possible, 1990 and 1999). Family comes first, then work, followed by friends, leisure, and finally by religion and politics. Each will be dealt with separately.

Table 1. Importance of domains in Europe

	West		East		South		North	
	'90	'99	'90	'99	'90	'99	'90	'99
Family	96	97	97	97	98	99	98	98
Friends	90	94	78	85	89	87	96	94
Work	90	89	93	91	95	99	98	98
Leisure	84	88	76	75	81	85	92	72
Religion	52	47	40	48	60	70	29	31
Politics	36	40	41	30	24	31	44	66

(source: EVS, 1990-1999, in %; very and quite important)

Though a series of surveys is needed if real changes are to be discovered (by comparing cohorts of age-groups), a comparison of age-groups in a single time period can at least indicate a trend. Table 2 offers such a comparison for Russia, Ukraine, Flanders, and Ireland.

The order of the domains according to their importance is mainly the same. But several differences strike the observer. Leisure is much more important in both Western countries. Indeed, under the given circumstances, people in the East have to work hard to survive. Moreover, it shows that one of the main differences between Western Europe, on the one hand, and the countries of Central and Eastern Europe, on the other, is the fact that in the latter work remains very important. A consumer society is typical for the West. In both the Eastern countries, religion has a different position in the mentality than in both the Western countries, religion being more important in Ukraine than in Russia, and in Ireland than in Belgium. Most important however is the accentuation of the family, which can be found in a more detailed analysis.

Table 2. Importance of domains in Russia, Ukraine, Flanders and Ireland

		Russia	*Ukraine*	*Flanders*	*Ireland*
Family	Age group				
	18-30	97	95	98	100
	31-45	97	97	95	100
	46-60	96	97	97	98
	61+	91	96	92	96
Friends	18-30	87	92	99	100
	31-45	84	89	93	96
	46-60	80	86	89	96
	61+	69	81	88	96
Work	18-30	92	91	90	92
	31-45	96	96	95	92
	46-60	89	89	89	86
	61+	52	54	76	61
Leisure	18-30	78	78	91	91
	31-45	76	75	93	88
	46-60	68	65	88	86
	61+	49	49	85	81
Religion	18-30	35	41	30	50
	31-45	39	49	32	65
	46-60	45	57	52	81
	60+	62	69	66	95
Politics	18-30	29	31	24	26
	31-45	37	40	34	31
	46-60	44	41	36	37
	60+	42	38	52	37

(source: EVS, 1999, in %)

3. Family and Marriage

The interviewees were asked to classify a list of 15 factors considered more or less important for a happy marriage. Table 3 presents an analysis of three of these factors. In most countries the quality of interpersonal relations is stressed most (respect, understanding, tolerance, faithfulness), to be followed by a happy sexual relationship, and then by children. Factors that were important in the past, such as belonging to the same social class, the same political orientation, or the same religion are steadily declining in importance. In the East, living apart from in-laws is also stressed, while it should be noted that housing is a problem.

Table 3. 'Factors important for a successful marriage'

	Age group	Russia	Ukraine	Flanders	Ireland
Faithfulness	18-30	62	70	95	94
	31-45	71	78	88	94
	46-60	74	81	88	95
	60+	80	87	90	98
Children	18-30	65	76	55	47
	31-45	76	86	56	61
	46-60	76	86	57	64
	60+	78	88	61	67
Same religious belief	18-30	8	18	12	8
	31-45	12	20	11	21
	46-60	11	24	19	29
	60+	17	34	31	54

(source: EVS, 1999, in %, 'very important')

For all three items a striking difference is observed between Russia and Ukraine. Faithfulness is more important in the Western countries, but children are considered more important in the Eastern ones. Nevertheless, no country in Europe reaches the population replacement level of 2.1 children per woman under the age of 45. The differences between the age groups are most striking in Ireland, where for the younger generations the secularisation process and post-traditionalism are, since the economic success in the country, an overwhelming phenomenon This process is much older in Belgium.

Answers to other questions reveal that changes in mentalities are occurring, at least in the younger generations, notwithstanding the high scores for the family. More and more people consider marriage to be an outdated institution. Comparative figures for the last decades in the West show that this is a phenomenon that is increasing in importance. Table 4 provides some information on current attitudes.

Table 4. "Marriage is an outdated institution"

	Age groups	Russia	Ukraine	Flanders	Ireland
Marriage outdated	18-30	32	28	27	28
	31-45	25	17	29	25
	46-60	15	15	28	18
	60+	10	11	18	16

(source: EVS, 1999, in %)

High divorce rates as well as women's emancipation and modern reproductive techniques support the opinion that a woman may have a child without a stable relationship with a man. This is a new phenomenon in the West as well as in the East. Again the trends are parallel, as is seen in Table 5. The situation in Flanders is about the same as in Russia. Ukraine follows Russia as Ireland is following Flanders.

Table 5. "A woman wants to be a single parent: do you find this acceptable?

		Russia	*Ukraine*	*Flanders*	*Ireland*
Woman single parent	Age group				
	18-30	60	46	56	44
	31-45	59	45	65	40
	46-60	54	41	54	24
	60+	37	24	37	19

(source: EVS, 1999, in %)

However, much more in Russia and Ukraine than in Flanders and Ireland, most people think that it is best for a child to grow up with both parents, as is apparent in Table 6.

Table 6. It is best for a child to grow up with both parents

		Russia	*Ukraine*	*Flanders*	*Ireland*
Best both parents	Age group				
	18-30	91	95	67	53
	31-45	95	95	67	53
	46-60	96	98	80	75
	60+	97	99	86	86

(source: EVS, 1999, in %)

The opinion of the parents about the education of their children is important for the future evolution of a society. In the survey, all were asked which qualities they consider important to teach their children at home. Interviewees had to select five items out of a list of eleven. Generally speaking, in the Western part of Europe three qualities are significantly mentioned first: tolerance, a feeling of responsibility, and good manners. For Ireland imagination is added, while a feeling of responsibility scores very low. In both the eastern countries hard work comes first, while good manners and tolerance are much less appreciated than in the West. This information on about eight selected qualities, appears in Table 7.

Table 7. Qualities to teach children at home

		Russia	Ukraine	Flanders	Ireland
	Age group				
Good manners	18-30	64	55	83	90
	31-45	59	58	80	84
	46-60	55	57	87	84
	60+	52	49	89	92
Responsibility	18-30	77	78	80	51
	31-45	77	74	84	47
	46-60	76	77	82	41
	60+	71	69	78	48
Tolerance and respect	18-30	63	61	78	73
	31-45	65	68	87	78
	46-60	70	65	87	78
	60+	70	64	78	70
Hard work	18-30	82	80	28	36
	31-45	91	91	17	29
	46-60	93	90	25	44
	60+	96	88	35	42
Thrift	18-30	45	42	38	16
	31-45	51	50	31	18
	46-60	51	47	41	23
	60+	58	60	50	29
Obedience	18-30	29	29	48	48
	31-45	29	36	40	42
	46-60	32	35	44	45
	60+	46	38	50	54
Imagination	18-30	11	12	27	67
	31-45	8	14	28	68
	46-60	4	9	17	83
	60+	3	5	18	83
Religious Faith	18-30	4	10	9	21
	31-45	7	22	10	34
	46-60	7	13	12	42
	60+	18	24	17	65

(source: EVS, 1999, in %)

4. Work

We have already seen that work is much more important in the East than in the West. In the East it is a question of survival, not in the least for women. In the West, people more consistently stress the expressive aspects of work, i.e., the qualitative aspects (like pleasant people to work with), while in the East the instrumental aspects (like good pay and having a job) are more important. Nevertheless, for the younger generations the importance of the expressive values increases (as, for instance, chances for promotion, utilising one's abilities).

Generally speaking, Ukraine is closer to the West than Russia. In Table 8 more details are given about six of the fifteen aspects of work presented to the interviewees.

Table 8. "Aspects of work, considered important"

		Russia	Ukraine	Flanders	Ireland
	Age group				
Good pay	18-30	92	92	86	91
	31-45	93	94	81	86
	46-60	88	92	83	89
	60+	82	73	82	87
Pleasant people	18-30	58	68	91	80
	31-45	55	65	84	71
	46-60	56	71	83	75
	60+	50	58	78	77
Job security	18-30	64	69	56	66
	31-45	74	76	45	65
	46-60	72	83	52	71
	60+	63	57	60	72
Promotion chances	18-30	44	46	56	56
	31-45	27	38	26	44
	45-60	25	42	31	47
	60+	19	28	43	54
Responsible job	18-30	25	32	39	53
	31-45	25	35	33	46
	46-60	28	45	30	56
	60+	25	27	39	59
Useful for Society	18-30	22	28	40	36
	31-45	22	26	35	36
	45-60	24	39	48	45
	60+	19	30	51	50

(source: EVS, 1999, in %)

In a 'capitalistic' society, promotion and competition are in high esteem. One of the questions raised tried to catch this aspect by asking if a secretary doing the same work as another one, but working quicker and more efficiently, should be paid more than the other secretary. Since 1981, in all the Western countries the opinion has steadily been more willing to give the quicker, more efficient worker higher pay. Thus inequality enters into the workplace. In Russia and in Ukraine this seems even more important than in the West (where all salaries are much higher). This is shown in Table 9.

Table 9. "Is it fair to pay a better secretary more than one who is not as efficient?"

		Russia	Ukraine	Flanders	Ireland
	Age group				
Fair to pay more	18-30	92	94	66	71
	31-45	94	93	66	63
	46-60	94	93	68	61
	60+	92	86	65	61

(source: EVS, 1999, in %)

In the West, a certain xenophobia influences people to prefer nationals to people from other countries when jobs are scarce. The same is true when one has a choice between men and women, though in both cases younger generations are more open and tolerant. This discrimination is also found in Russia and Ukraine, though here the differences between the generations are not significant. It strikes the observer that women are still discriminated against, notwithstanding the fact that the participation of women as workers is traditionally higher in the East than in the West, as is apparent from Table 10.

Table 10. "Discrimination against foreigners and women for work"

		Russia	Ukraine	Flanders	Ireland
	Age groups				
Nationals priority	18-30	69	67	58	67
	31-45	72	70	57	69
	46-60	71	68	64	74
	60+	80	74	69	82
Men priority	18-30	37	25	6	3
	31-45	36	30	19	11
	46-60	36	33	20	17
	60+	35	34	40	35

(source: EVS, 1999, in %)

In this context it seems interesting to consider the opinions of the people concerning what they hope will happen in the future. Interviewees were asked if certain changes seem good or bad. The following answers on a longer list give an insight into what people find good. The East is clearly more 'materialist' (Inglehart). It puts significantly more stress on money, work, technology and less of a natural lifestyle than the West does. All four countries want more attention given to the family, but the East is more concerned about the development of the individual than the West, doubtless because people have fewer chances in the East. On both sides, the majority of people want somewhat more authority, of course in a very different socio-political climate for East and West. Many in the East seem unhappy with centralisation and want more power for local authorities (see Table 11).

Table 11. "Changes considered desirable in the future"

	Age group	Russia	Ukraine	Flanders	Ireland
Emphasis on individual	18-30	93	97	78	90
	31-45	92	91	80	94
	46-60	89	92	81	91
	60+	90	96	75	89
Emphasis on family	18-30	89	86	80	90
	30-45	94	87	81	95
	46-60	96	95	86	96
	60+	95	93	91	97
Emphasis on Technology	18-30	87	89	46	72
	31-45	88	88	54	66
	46-60	89	92	51	70
	60+	87	88	50	70
More natural lifestyle	18-30	58	55	66	70
	31-45	58	63	79	84
	46-60	59	72	82	89
	60+	60	66	87	88
More respect for authority	18-30	50	55	50	66
	31-45	53	62	54	71
	46-60	60	71	60	82
	60+	64	67	73	89
Less emphasis on money	18-30	44	45	56	65
	31-45	45	40	65	68
	46-60	43	43	66	72
	60+	50	49	61	70
Decrease importance of work	18-30	22	26	33	42
	31-45	15	23	40	39
	46-60	13	18	34	37
	60+	10	15	30	26
More power for local authorities	18-30	43	50	20	33
	31-45	53	49	20	43
	46-60	57	67	27	56
	60+	66	63	25	61

(source: EVS, 1999, in %)

5. Ethics

All domains of life are influenced by the ethical standards of the people. In the West as well as in the East the older generations find, much more than the younger ones, that clear and absolute guidelines concerning good and evil should always be followed. Younger generations claim that the circumstances are decisive for good and evil; for them, 'situation ethics' prevail. The general trend in the West accentuates the latter. Table 12 gives a comparative picture. Still more than in the previous data, the age effect is important.

Table 12. *"Absolute clear guidelines for good and evil or the circumstances?"*

		Russia	Ukraine	Flanders	Ireland
	Age group				
Clear guidelines	18-30	28	32	19	34
	31-45	39	44	27	34
	46-60	42	43	33	41
	60+	46	52	37	49

(source: EVS, 1999, in % for 'clear guidelines')

The survey tries to dig deeper into the ethical attitudes regarding a great number of different kinds of behaviour. Answers are on a scale of 1 (never justified) to 10 (always justified) concerning what people thought about these behaviours. The trend is more or less the same everywhere, (though Belgium is significantly more tolerant for euthanasia and homosexuality). Everywhere, people are more severe about property than about sexuality and more tolerant for abortion. In order to avoid too many figures, only overall national scores are given, omitting the age groups. However, everywhere the younger generations are more tolerant than the older ones.

Table 13. *"Permissiveness scores (1= never justified; 10= always justified) for a series of behaviours"*

	Russia	Ukraine	Belgium	Ireland
Joyriding	1.3	1.4	1.1	1.1
Driving under influence of alcohol	1.4	1.5	1.6	1.4
Accept a bribe	1.8	2.0	1.9	1.4
Littering	1.5	1.7	1.4	1.7
Speeding	2.0	2.2	2.2	1.8
Adultery	2.6	2.4	2.5	1.8
Claiming state benefits you are not entitled to	2.3	2.8	2.3	2.9
Taking soft drugs	1.3	1.3	1.6	1.9
Smoking in public places	3.0	3.1	2.9	3.3
Suicide	2.1	1.9	2.0	3.2
Cheating on tax	3.1	3.4	3.6	2.1
Lying in own interest	3.4	2.8	3.9	2.9
Having casual sex	2.8	2.7	2.6	2.7
Paying cash to avoid taxes	3.2	2.9	4.4	2.9
Abortion	4.7	3.8	4.3	2.9
Euthanasia (terminally ill)	5.6	5.2	5.9	3.3
Homosexuality	2.1	2.3	5.3	4.6
Divorce	5.0	4.5	5.5	4.8

(source: EVS, 1999, in scores)

On abortion, two questions were added for particular cases. The differences between East and West here are much clearer than in Table 13, Ireland being more reticent than Belgium, and both being more reticent than Russia or Ukraine. The availability of reliable contraceptives and bad housing are some of the reasons explaining the gap (see Table 14).

Table 14. "Approve abortion when the woman is not married or when the couple does not want more children"

		Russia	Ukraine	Flanders	Ireland
	Age group				
Woman not married	18-30	69	62	31	30
	30-45	62	53	46	21
	46-60	62	52	40	13
	60+	45	34	31	6
Not wanting children	18-30	81	68	22	24
	30-45	79	66	43	19
	45-60	77	66	30	10
	60+	57	44	17	5

(source: EVS, 1999, in %)

Of course, opinions about behaviour and actual behaviour do not always coincide. Therefore a question was added about what people think about the actual behaviour of their compatriots. Table 15 offers some insight into these opinions, which are clearly more negative than the personal opinions. Civic sense seems rather weak everywhere.

Table 15. "According to you, how many of our compatriots do the following?"

		Russia	Ukraine	Belgium	Ireland
Claim state benefits	almost all	2	1	5	3
	many	38	45	25	49
Cheat on tax	almost all	12	9	18	12
	many	56	58	48	51
Pay in cash...	almost all	9	7	12	11
	many	53	52	44	48
Taking soft drugs	almost all	1	-	-	2
	many	38	35	21	46
Littering	almost all	18	12	3	16
	many	57	53	33	54
Driving under influence of alcohol	almost all	2	1	1	4
	many	40	40	32	42
Have casual sex	almost all	6	5	1	8
	many	49	50	24	61

(source: EVS, 1999, in %)

The trust people say they have in their compatriots is an index for civic sense in general and for ethical behaviour in particular. The surveys confirm a gap between the Nordic countries (Protestants) and the other ones (be they sociologically Roman Catholic or Orthodox)[5]. Table 16 gives an indication of the responses to the saying that "one cannot be too careful in trusting others". Comparative surveys show the link between trust and economic performance.

Table 16. "Trust in people: one cannot be too careful"

		Russia	*Ukraine*	*Flanders*	*Ireland*
Cannot be too careful	Age group				
	18-30	78	73	57	69
	31-45	77	74	56	60
	46-60	74	71	61	62
	60+	75	71	67	66

(source: EVS, 1999, in %)

6. Politics

Even the superficial observer will admit that the West has a democratic tradition which for a long time has not existed in the East, and that the lack of this tradition has repercussions on all aspects of political life in the East. We will develop this theme in somewhat more detail because it is so important for the present time and for the future.

Trust in institutions is a good starting point, since this is the backbone of civil society. Interpreting the data is not simple. At face value, the various opinions may seem the same. However, underlying them are very different experiences of democracy. Some expect too much, others too little. Opinions may change overnight for the simple reason that an event – even one that is not typical at all, such as a crisis in the European Commission or the dioxin crisis in Belgium – can influence the mentality of the day. The figures show how fragile a democracy can be.

In the East, particularly, the high scores for the army and the church are striking. Both are symbols of an awakening national identity. However, according to the 1990 survey in the US, the church and the army (together with the police) scored highest for confidence given to institutions. A Russian survey showed confidence in the church to be higher in 1995 than in 1999: indeed people expected too much from a church weakened by decades of severe persecution. In the West, the situation is very diversified. In the Nordic countries, France, and the United Kingdom, the army rates very high, while the church scores rather low. In Italy, where the army is in low esteem, the church continues to receive a great deal of confidence from the people, who usually show little confidence in anything which has to do with the state. In Belgium and in Ireland, the church has lost a lot of confidence during the last two decades; (in the youngest age group it receives only 21% in Belgium and 30% in Ireland, compared with respectively 54% and 81% for those above the age of 60).

Table 17. "Trust in institutions"

	Russia	*Ukraine*	*Belgium*	*Ireland*
Educational system	71	71	79	86
Police	29	32	55	84
Civil service	37	38	43	59
Army	66	69	36	58
Justice system	36	32	34	54
Health care system	46	47	81	57
Parliament	17	27	34	31
European Union	25	45	43	60
United Nations	26	55	40	62
Church	61	65	40	51
Trade unions	30	37	35	46
Press	30	46	36	34

(source: EVS, 1999, in %, taking 'very much confidence' and 'quite a lot' together)

People everywhere trust their education system as a guarantee for the future. This is also the case for the health care and social security systems in Belgium and in its neighbouring countries, systems which score significantly lower in the East. The parliament rates low everywhere, though the meaning of this fact is rather different in the East than in the West. Ukraine is much more interested in the European Union than Russia is, and it also expresses more confidence in the United Nations. Trade unions, press, and justice systems do not receive much confidence anywhere. All in all, one can conclude that – with the exception of the army in the East – among the four countries considered it is only in Ireland that the state enjoys real confidence. Here Ireland seems to follow the Nordic Protestant countries.

But what do the people of these four countries really think about democracy? The differences between the two Western countries, on the one hand, and the two eastern ones, on the other, reflect aspects of the long previous history of the two groups. Table 18 shows how far people are satisfied (very or rather) with the way democracy is developing in their country. Ukraine seems a little more satisfied than Russia, and in both countries the younger generations claim more satisfaction, though the satisfied remain a small minority.

Table 18. "Satisfaction with democracy"

	Russia	Ukraine	Belgium	Ireland
very, rather satisfied	7	15	46	53

(source: EVS, 1999, 'very' and 'rather' satisfied, in %)

Nevertheless, most people consider democracy the best way of governing a people (Table 19). In Russia, however, (though not in Ukraine), people above the age of 45 have a negative opinion about the democratic system as such. They feel a nostalgia for what they consider to be the central characteristics of the previous system: security and stability.

Table 19. "The democratic system is the best"

	Russia	Ukraine	Belgium	Ireland
agree strongly, agree	53	84	85	90

(source: EVS, 1999, 'strongly agree' and 'agree', in %)

This means that people are criticising democracy as it actually works. Democracy often seems weak in the economic domain, as though it were indecisive and unable to keep order. Table 20 illustrates these criticisms. In Belgium, the Flemish are much more positive than the Walloons.

Table 20. "Democracy causes a bad economy, is indecisive and cannot maintain order"

	Russia	Ukraine	Belgium	Ireland
weak in economics	54	36	29	19
indecisive	72	54	54	39
cannot maintain order	65	50	35	22

(source: EVS, 1999, 'agree strongly', 'agree', in %)

The nostalgia for the past is typical for the East. Answers about the best way to govern a country express this nostalgia. Once again, the differences between East and West are striking. People were asked if they preferred a strong leader who does not have to worry about parliamentarian elections, or having experts in charge instead of a government, or even the possibility of giving the government over to the army. Table 21 is an eye-opener. Though in the East the army as an institution scores very high, only a small minority is in favour of entrusting the country to such a body.

Table 21. "Preferences for leadership in the country"

	Russia	Ukraine	Belgium	Ireland
a strong leader	49	59	31	26
experts in charge	51	50	20	38
army ruling	19	13	4	4

(source: EVS, 199, 'very good', 'good', in %)

In democratic regimes people honour freedom and endeavour to safeguard the respect for human rights. At the same time they want all citizens to enjoy a basic equality. This tension between freedom and equality is typical for democracies and it traditionally characterises the split between more liberal and more socio-democratic parties. The survey reveals the general trends in public opinion (Table 22). In Belgium, Flanders prefers freedom, Wallonia equality. The score concerning human rights is also higher in Flanders than in Wallonia.

Table 22. "Equality and freedom are both important, but if you had to choose between the two, which would you choose? Is there respect for human rights in your country at the present time (a lot of respect, some respect)?"

	Russia	Ukraine	Belgium	Ireland
freedom above equality	47	53	45	49
equality above freedom	47	41	47	44
human rights respected	16	22	62	76

(source: EVS, 1999, in %)

Sociologists usually make a distinction between the state and civil society. Government decisions normally should reflect the general concerns of civil society. The state should provide a framework for the development of free movements and organisations. The state also should promote the coexistence of people with different attitudes regarding social relations. Several questions dealt with this area of civil society. During the Soviet regime, people were forced to become members of youth groups, unions, and cultural organisations. Today, as a consequence, people have become very reticent. Moreover, the stress of working hard for survival allows little opportunity for leisure and membership in movements. Looking at the European map, for instance, we find that membership in volunteer organisations is much more widely spread in Northern Europe than in the rest of the continent. Table 23 gives comparative information. For fifteen different organisations and activities, the interviewees were asked a) if they are members of such organisations and b) if they are in fact active in them. Again, the differences are striking, particularly when we take into account the fact that in Russia active membership and participation in organisations relates mainly to the trade unions.

Table 23. "Membership and active involvement in volunteer organisations and activities"

	Russia	Ukraine	Flanders	Ireland
membership	32	34	80	57
active involvement	8	12	50	31

(source: EVS, 1999, in %)

A second example deals with attitudes regarding 'unwanted neighbours'. Comparisons have to take into account the bad housing in Russia and Ukraine, the fact that Belgium is a country with open borders and that Ireland is an island. A distinction is made between two kinds of neighbours: firstly, the so-called 'deviants' and, secondly, people belonging to another race or religion. In the East, the differences between the generations are rather small and insignificant; in the two Western regions, younger people are much more tolerant. Walloons seem less xenophobic than Flemings on this point (Table 24).

Table 24. "Negative attitudes regarding 'unwanted neighbours"

	Russia	Ukraine	Flanders	Ireland
Heavy drinkers	73	72	48	32
People with criminal records	57	72	35	55
Left-wing extremists	23	35	38	33
Right-wing extremists	21	36	45	32
Drug addicts	84	88	52	65
People with aids	52	59	17	22
Homosexuals	58	65	18	26
Gypsies	45	52	39	25
Immigrants, foreign workers	11	15	25	12
Muslims	13	24	27	13
Jews	11	10	18	11

(source: EVS, 1999, in %)

Another question within this context dealt with attitudes regarding state intervention. On a ten-point scale, people had to indicate their opinions on the following issues: a) whether they should personally be more responsible for themselves or whether it is the state's responsibility to take care of them; b) whether unemployed people should have to accept any available job (and, if not, lose state support) or whether they should have the right to refuse a job they do not like; c) whether the state should give more freedom to enterprises or exercise more control over them; d) whether economic competition is good or bad. Table 25 gives the answers in terms of scores and shows that the differences are often insignificant.

Table 25. "Attitudes regarding state intervention"

	Russia	Ukraine	Belgium	Ireland
State is responsible	5.7	6.0	5.1	4.4
Take any job available	6.1	6.2	4.8	5.6
State should control firms	6.0	5.4	5.6	5.0
Competition is harmful	4.0	4.0	3.7	4.0

(source: EVS, 1999, in scores on a ten-point scale)

A last series of questions dealt with a list of aims to be pursued by society. People had a choice between: a) maintain order; b) give people more say in important government decisions; c) fight rising prices; d) protect freedom of speech. Table 26 specifies the answers. Once again in the East people are primarily concerned about security in an often chaotic social situation.

Table 26. Aims for society

	Russia	Ukraine	Belgium	Ireland
Maintain order	56	54	37	37
Give people more say	18	24	24	36
Fighting rising prices	23	39	16	18
Protect freedom of speech	1	9	19	8

(source: EVS, 1999, in %)

7. Religion

Though the results seem to support the general conclusion that religion is more important than politics, it must be recognised that religion and church have different meanings in the four societies studied here. In the East the link with the state is strong, but the persecution of religion and its consequences as well as the previous ambiguous relation between church and state still influence the mentality. In Belgium, society is very much secularised. In Ireland people remain very religious, although after the enormous economic progress the country has enjoyed in recent years, the secularisation process is speeding up. This results in great differences between the four societies, in particular when age groups are taken into account. Everywhere a substantial majority says they are religious people (Table 27).

Table 27. "Are you religious or not?"

		Russia	*Ukraine*	*Flanders*	*Ireland*
	Age group				
Religious people	18-30	63	77	62	68
	31-45	62	69	65	68
	46-60	61	78	78	80
	60+	78	78	85	86
Convinced atheists	18-30	4	2	3	1
	31-45	4	3	7	5
	46-60	6	3	2	-
	60+	4	2	1	-

(source: EVS, 1999, in %)

In the East, as well as in the West, convinced atheists form only a tiny minority. Most people want religious ceremonies to mark the important moments of life, even if these ceremonies are often more an expression of belonging to a traditional 'Christendom' rather than of believing in 'Christianity' (Table 28).

Table 28. 'Want a religious ceremony at birth, marriage and death'

		Russia	*Ukraine*	*Flanders*	*Ireland*
	Age group				
At birth	18-30	74	83	71	88
	31-45	75	84	62	87
	46-60	69	86	72	92
	60+	82	87	83	96
At marriage	18-30	51	64	69	90
	31-45	47	66	57	87
	46-60	50	71	72	93
	60+	70	72	83	98
At death	18-30	78	84	76	95
	31-45	78	85	65	92
	46-60	75	84	76	96
	60+	84	86	87	99

(source: EVS, 1999, in %)

Christianity has to do with beliefs. Looking at the answers concerning the beliefs of the people, we see that (belief in God somehow excepted) people believe much less than their desire for ceremonies would imply. Moreover, their belief in God needs to be qualified. Only a minority of people (Ireland excepted) believe that God is a person. On a ten-point scale concerning the importance given to God, Russians register 5.2, Ukrainians 6.3, Flemish 5.1 and Irish 7.4. Secondly, in all four cases the younger generations believe less than their grandparents. As Russia differs from Ukraine, Flanders differs from Ireland (Table 29).

Table 29. Beliefs

	Russia	*Ukraine*	*Flanders*	*Ireland*
God	70	80	66	95
Life after death	36	40	37	78
Hell	35	38	14	53
Heaven	36	40	28	85
Sin	68	74	39	86
Reincarnation	32	28	16	23
Telepathy	58	56	37	34
Personal God	32	41	25	63
Spirit or life force	18	25	40	25

(source: EVS, 1999, in %)

In Russia, 50% declare that they belong to a religious denomination, 91% of whom are Orthodox and 6% of whom are Muslim. In Ukraine, 56% belong to a religious denomination, 74% of whom belong to one of the three Orthodox churches and 15% of whom belong to the two Roman Catholic rites. In Flanders 63% say they belong to a religious denomination (59% Roman Catholics), and in Ireland 90% (95% of whom are Roman Catholics). Belonging is not the same as believing, nor is believing the same as practising one's religion. Table 30 shows the percentage who attend church at least once a month and how many go to church less than once a year or never.

Table 30. "Attend services at least once a month, or else less than once a year or never"

	Russia	*Ukraine*	*Flanders*	*Ireland*
At least once a month	9	16	30	67
Practically never	50	30	45	10

(source: EVS, 1999, in %)

Churches are related to the civil society. The interviewees had to answer a question concerning their opinions about answers given by the churches to their personal moral problems, family problems, social questions, and spiritual needs (Table 31). The answers are disturbing. In the Orthodox area people are seldom in the church, many do not even belong to a religious denomination and Orthodoxy has developed a social doctrine, yet nevertheless a great majority find answers in their church for moral problems and spiritual needs.

Table 31. "In how far are the churches answering questions and needs?"

	Russia	Ukraine	Flanders	Ireland
Moral problems	70	80	24	30
Family problems	55	63	23	27
Social questions	25	30	24	27
Spiritual needs	74	82	41	63

(source: EVS, 1999, in %)

8. Conclusion

Every observer of social life in Russia and Ukraine admits the obvious differences with Western Europe, particularly in the areas of politics and economics. The previous paragraphs did not touch on the question of preferences for political parties. These preferences have been inquired into in Russia for more than 13 major parties among the about 150 registered and in Ukraine for more than 23 parties. Of course, the abnormal number of parties is astonishing and symbolizes the chaotic situation. Moreover, most major parties are conservative and nationalist. In the Western countries one normally finds only two to six parties, with a left-right divide. This nationalism is also revealed in the great trust people claim to have in the church and the army. It is clear that our Eastern neighbours fear chaos, and it is for this reason that they stress the maintenance of order and a strong leadership. As in the long past, they yearn for some form of paternalism. Nevertheless, as in the West, a great majority consider the democratic system the best way for governing a country. Far more than in the Western regions, the East is struck by the weaknesses of a democratic regime it dreams about but does not enjoy. Indeed, the great expectations fostered by the celebrated watchword 'perestroika' – and still evident in a 1995 survey – have turned into disillusion.

For security, people turn to family and church. Values such as friendship and comradeship also play an important role in their lives. Out of sheer necessity, work is much more important in the East. Though socialism is the official ideology, trust in practically all government and official institutions is very low. There is a visible fatigue in society, caused by endless political debates. Most people are unwilling to accept responsibility. In the East, at the grass roots level, society seems much less active than in the West: membership in movements and active involvement in volunteer organisations are very low.

On both sides, however, people are looking for a more just society. On this point, the differences are not significant. In the survey, people were confronted with three themes relating to a more just society: 'the elimination of extreme inequalities in income between citizens', 'guaranteeing that basic needs are met for all (in terms of food, housing, clothes, education, health)' and 'social and financial recognition for people on the basis of their merits'. Table 32 presents the results.

Table 32. "Desire for a more 'just' society"

	Russia	Ukraine	Flanders	Ireland
Eliminating extreme inequalities	74	59	70	68
Guaranteeing basic needs	97	93	91	95
Recognition based on merits	92	83	79	83

(source: EVS, 1999, 'very important' and 'quite important', in %)

Nevertheless, a deeper look into the minds of the eastern interviewees reveals many parallels with the two western countries (and with the West in general). Although the family scores highest in the areas examined, for about a third of the population the institution of marriage seems outdated. As in the West, divorce is approved by the majority of people. In the permissiveness scale, differences between the four countries are also small, with the exception of abortion, where the East is clearly more tolerant – a fact which is mainly explained by poverty. On the other hand, the West no longer discriminates against homosexuality. In the East, as well as in the West, people primarily want more concern for the development of the individual and for strengthening the family, though in the West the so-called 'post-materialist' values are in higher esteem.

Where in the West – particularly in matters of religion and ethics – differences between generations (i. e. between those born before and after World War II) are often enormous, this is much less the case in both Eastern countries. For the two issues mentioned, civil society in the West is understood to be caught up in a process of accelerated secularisation. All this means that, notwithstanding enormous gaps, there are a number of undeniable convergencies between East and West which cannot be denied. Neither can we deny that people in the West seem more happy and satisfied than people in the East, as is shown in Table 33.

Table 33. 'Life and job satisfaction'

	Russia	Ukraine	Flanders	Ireland
Life satisfaction	4.7	4.5	7.7	8.1
Job satisfaction	6.1	5.8	7.6	7.8

(source: EVS, 1999, in scores: 1= not satisfied at all, 10= absolutely satisfied)

It is hoped that the fourth wave of the *European Values Study*, foreseen for 2008, will allow an assessment that enables a true comparison not only of the situation of the two Eastern countries with that of certain Western regions, but also a deeper look into trends. We are all more and more in "the same boat" and will increasingly have to develop a common future together.

Notes

1   Joll J. *The Unspoken Assumptions,* 1914. Quoted in: Robert D English, *Russia and the Idea of the West, Gorbatchev, Intellectuals, and the End of the Cold War.* New York, Columbia University Press, 2000.
2   The Foundation *European Values Study* is located at the University of Tilburg in the Netherlands. Its Website is: http://www.evs.kub.nl.
3   Ester P., Halman L., and Rukavishnikov V. *From Cold War to Cold Peace? A Comparative Empirical Study of Russian and Western Political Cultures.* Tilburg University Press, 1997.
4   Here I wish to thank Ms. Elena Bashkirova, General Director of the Research Group Romir in Moscow, who organised the survey in Russia and has sent me her comments. For this article only the author is responsible.
5   Alain Peyrefitte, *La Société de Confiance, Essai sur les origines et la nature du développement,* Ed. Paris, Odile Jacob, 1995.

Russia, the Countries 'In-between' and Europe's Dual Enlargement

John Löwenhardt

After the demise of Communism, contemporary Europe has three types of states. All of them now have a voice in the two most inclusive institutions, the Organisation for Security and Co-operation in Europe and (with the unique exception of Belarus) the Council of Europe. But in respect of institutions that really matter for prosperity and security, the European Union and NATO, membership is much more exclusive. First are those who are current member states and who jointly decide whether and how fast the EU and NATO are to be enlarged. These are currently the 15 EU member states and 19 members of NATO, two of them non-European. Only three Central European states are currently included in one of the two: Poland, Hungary and the Czech Republic, which were admitted to NATO in March 1999.

The second group of countries are those for whom inclusion is a real perspective, the 'pre-ins'. Some of them have entered NATO, others expect to be admitted and all are in a process of negotiation with the European Commission concerning their accession to the EU. Even though the accession process is slowing down due to various complications and many of the 'pre-ins' cannot hope to accede in the near future, the prospect of EU membership (and the concrete preparations for the adoption of the EU-*acquis*) can be argued to have a beneficial impact on these Central European societies.

The third and final group consists of countries where, due to a lack of information on the character and mode of operation of these institutions, sections of their populations and élite show unrealistic expectations of being included in 'European structures'. These are the countries that are being tormented by failed or stalling transformation: Russia, Belarus, Ukraine, and Moldova. In reality the widened gap between these four countries and their immediate neighbours to the West has created the prospect of them being shut out of 'Fortress Europe'. With growing despair, populations in these countries look at the successes of their Western neighbours and fear that they will soon be separated and from the rest of Europe by a forbidding Schengen Wall.

In this contribution, issues of European identity and views of the EU and NATO among the populations and elite of these four 'permanent outsiders' will be briefly looked at. But first we should look at their current situation, their similarities and differences, starting with the dominant power in the East, Russia.

Russia is a Eurasian power, and it is important to realise that it has interests in both Europe and Asia. But under Vladimir Putin it has said farewell to its big power aspirations. A recent study on attitudes among the Russian foreign policy élite has found that the number of those who think that in the foreseeable future Russia might become one of the top five developed nations is only 40 per cent of what it was in 1993. During the same period the number of those who think Russia should turn away from global ambitions and concentrate on its domestic problems has risen six-fold.[1] The new president has captured this mood and under his reign Europe has moved up in foreign policy priorities. The relationship with the US has clearly been downgraded in importance. The deepening of its integration with European structures and policies – including its emerging military role – is currently one of the main instruments by which Russian authorities hope to support two goals: (1) economic recovery, and (2) the frustration of American efforts to sustain what the Russians see as a 'unipolar world'.

The remaining three countries are of a different order. Belarus, Ukraine and Moldova have a lot in common. They are classic borderlands that over past centuries have been moved back and forth between their neighbours. The new states on these lands did not fix their own borders – they had to accept the administrative borders of the collapsing USSR. Ten years ago, these countries had no 'abroad' of their own, and no foreign policy. National identity was – and remains – unsettled. In all three, the modern state is a comparatively new phenomenon, with resulting elementary problems of state building. Russia under Putin seems to be regaining its composure, however difficult the economic situation may be. But at the beginning of the 21st century the 'lands-in-between' are still very much in crisis, and uncertain about both domestic and foreign policy orientations. One parameter stands out, and is widely realised by both populations and élite in all three countries: they are and, for the foreseeable future, will remain highly dependent on Russia for trade and energy.

What do the political classes in the 'states-in-between' see when they look East and West? To the East, in Russia they see a new pragmatism of President Putin, who has left Yeltsin's romantic and unpredictable foreign policy far behind. Since early 2000 Russia is increasingly focusing on its bilateral relations with its immediate western neighbours, stressing that in these relations there must be a *'balans interesov'* (balance of interests). Russia is using economic levers (such as stakes in Belarusian and Ukrainian firms) to redress the imbalance left behind by Yeltsin. The appointment, in May 2001, of Viktor Chernomyrdin as Russian ambassador to Kiev underlined this development.

If they look to the West, the leaders in Minsk, Kiev and Chisinau first see a Central Europe that has made great progress in its recovery from Communist domination. They see basic political stability and, from their perspective, economic affluence. The estimated average level of GDP in the CIS countries in 1998 stood at only 53 per cent of 1989. For Russia it was 55, for Belarus 78, Ukraine 37 and for Moldova a mere 32 per cent. But in the same year Slovakia stood at 100 per cent, the Czech Republic and Hungary at 95 and Poland at 117 per cent.[2] They see states that are negotiating their accession with the European Commission and have in three cases entered NATO more than two years ago. And they also see a forbidding Schengen Wall looming up and threatening to cut them off from the rest of Europe.

Beyond Central Europe they see the prosperous and stable EU, with 20 per cent of world's GDP; just one per cent behind the US. They see a European capital, Brussels, where Eurocrats and diplomats show increasing signs of fatigue with the impossible East Europeans.

1. European Identity

Now to move to questions of identity. These, after all, are the cultural structures underlying foreign policy orientation and in the end those who make foreign policy cannot ignore them. How European are these societies after all? In the national opinion surveys that we commissioned in all four countries we included a simple question on European identity, by asking respondents whether they ever felt European. The results showed a striking difference between Russia and Belarus on the one hand, and Ukraine and Moldova on the other.

Table 1: Perceptions of European Identity (column percentages)

	Russia	Belarus	Ukraine	Moldova
Often	18	16	8	9
Sometimes	34	34	26	25
Rarely/never	47	38	57	56
Don't know	2	12	8	10

The question wording was: 'Do you think of yourself as a European?'

Source: National surveys commissioned by the 'Outsiders' project, Belarus ('Novak' market and opinion research) 13 – 27 April 2000, N=1,090, adult population aged 18+; Moldova (Independent Sociological Service 'Opinia') 13 – 19 February 2000, sample on territory between Prut and Dnestr: not including Prinestrov'e and Bendery, N=1,000, adult population 18+; Russia (Russian Centre for the Study of Public Opinion VTsIOM) 19 – 29 January 2000, N=1,940, population 16+; Ukraine (Kiev International Institute of Sociology) 18 February – 3 March 2000, N=1,592.

In the first two countries, 50 to 52 percent said they often or sometimes felt European, whereas in Ukraine and Moldova the percentage was only 34 (see Table 1). Paradoxically, the identity of Russia, the country that straddles the frontier between Europe and Asia, is more European than that of Ukraine and

Moldova which both claim to be located close to 'the heart of Europe'. This may well be a consequence of Russia's location and of its historical ties with France and Germany in particular. Russian cultural history, for more than a century, has seen a struggle between 'Westernizers' and 'Slavophiles', a philosophical debate that has left its marks on the psyche of contemporary Russians and Belarussians. Conversely, in its Soviet incarnation, Russia – seen as the core of the USSR – really mattered to Western Europe. Ukraine and Moldova were virtually unknown. For whatever it is worth, in interviews, contemporary Russians time and again recall the degree to which they felt that their country was respected by the rest of the world, including Europe – until the USSR collapsed. During that same century, the 'significant others' of Ukraine and Moldova, on the other hand, were Russia to the East, and Central European countries such as Poland, Hungary and Romania to the West. European identity in these two countries is of very recent origin, and highly superficial.

2. The EU and EU Enlargement

On the issue of the EU and its enlargement, these two sets of countries show differences as well. Belarus is very much tied to Russia by its Union with that country (stipulating, amongst others, co-ordination of their foreign policies) and paralysed vis-à-vis Europe for as long as Lukashenko is in power. Russia, with Belarus in train, is the big outside power in the enlargement game between Brussels and the capitals of Central Europe. But in Kiev and Chisinau, the EU is largely a wishful dream. Integration with the EU is often little more than a panacea for the chronic ills that these societies and their political classes suffer. As a deputy foreign minister of Moldova said to us in July 2000: 'nine years of independence have shown us our impotence in dealing with our own affairs. We now need *constructive pressure* from the EU to *set things in motion*' in Moldova.[3] Approaching Europe is, in the words of former president Lucinschi's adviser on foreign policy, a way 'to solve all our problems'.[4]

Ten years after independence the problems have only grown and Ukraine and Moldova are still in crisis. Ultimately the reason for their failed transition must be sought in their political schizophrenia, the inability to make a firm and uncompromising choice between East or West – an inability that is related to their weak and unsettled national identity.[5] Both have been courting the European Union, and at the same time have seen an increase in their economic dependence on Russia. Their states show strong signs of failure – how else to interpret, for example, the report that one third of the Moldovan workforce is abroad.[6] Developments in 2000-2001 – the crisis surrounding President Kuchma, the fall of Prime-Minister Yushchenko (April 2001), the communist victory in Moldova, and last but not least the pragmatism of Vladimir Putin – have favoured Russian influence on these countries.

And yet, in spite of all this, we have found that one of the main concerns in Eastern Europe is the idea of being cut-off from their Central European neighbours and Western Europe by the new Schengen wall. A recent report by the Batory Foundation aptly noted that the open borders policy of the 1990s, encouraged by West European states, has contributed to the overcoming of prejudice and stereotypes in Central and Eastern Europe.[7] It would give an entirely wrong signal if as a result of EU enlargement the eastern border would be hermetically sealed.

3. NATO and NATO Enlargement

On NATO and its enlargement, too, Ukraine and Moldova stand apart from Russia and Belarus. Their élite show a relatively benign attitude towards NATO, and in fact military co-operation between Ukraine, Moldova, and NATO has been strengthened.[8] But within the Russian and Belarusian élite (with the exception of the Belarusian opposition and a very small section of Moscow's political and business élite) concern about the expansion of the Euro-Atlantic alliance is strong. Except for paper declarations, NATO and its leaders have done very little indeed to dispel their old stereotypes. On the contrary, by their bombing of Serbia and simultaneous enlargement in the spring of 1999, they have strengthened such stereotypes. To President Lukashenko they provided hard evidence in support of his anti-Western rhetoric.

In relation to this use of anti-NATO rhetoric at the élite level, it is remarkable that popular attitudes toward NATO expansion are rather subdued. There are clear differences between Russia and Belarus on one hand, and Ukraine-Moldova on the other, but the differences are certainly not black and white. Analysis of the surveys that we commissioned in all four countries shows that the threat perception of past or future NATO expansion is consistently lower in Ukraine-Moldova than in Russia-Belarus (Tables 2-3). In Belarus and Russia, one quarter to one third of the population see further expansion of NATO as a threat or as very to fairly harmful to their country. In Moldova and Ukraine this is only 11 to 14 percent (Table 3). But remarkably, in spite of the more aggressive wording of the question in the Russian survey, some 28 percent of Russians do not see expansion of NATO to the Baltic States as a threat, and over one third of them are unable to provide an answer at all.

Table 2: Threat perception from 1999 NATO expansion (Poland, Hungary, Czech Republic) in four 'Outsider' states, 2000, column percentages.

	Russia	Belarus	Ukraine	Moldova
Big threat	6.3 (6.5)	4.0 (3.4)	2.0 (1.6)	2.8 (1.6)
Some threat	22.0 (21.8)	15.9 (15.0)	7.2 (6.2)	12.5 (12.1)
Big or some threat	28.3 (28.3)	19.9 (18.4)	9.2 (7.8)	15.3 (13.7)
Little threat	16.7 (17.1)	35.1 (35.0)	28.4 (29.5)	21.4 (20.3)
No threat at all	18.6 (18.6)	24.4 (23.5)	41.9 (41.9)	44.5 (49.6)
Little or no threat	35.3 (35.7)	59.5 (58.5)	70.3 (71.4)	65.9 (69.9)
Don't know	36.5 (36.0)	20.5 (23.1)	20.5 (20.9)	18.8 (16.4)
Total	100	100	100	100

Score for total population (score for main population group). The question was: 'After the collapse of the Soviet Union the Czech Republic, Hungary and Poland became member of NATO. Do you think this presents a threat to our country?' *Source*: as Table 1.

Table 3: Threat perception from future NATO expansion in four 'Outsider' states, 2000, column percentages.

	Russia	Belarus	Ukraine	Moldova
Very harmful	14.4 (15.1)	5.8 (5.3)	3.8 (3.8)	3.6 (2.3)
Fairly harmful	22.4 (22.3)	22.1 (21.1)	10.1 (9.5)	7.3 (6.3)
Very or fairly harmful	36.8 (37.4)	27.9 (26.4)	13.9 (13.3)	10.9 (8.6)
Not very harmful	12.1 (11.6)	28.6 (28.7)	27.1 (27.2)	22.3 (22.9)
Not at all harmful	16.5 (16.7)	19.2 (18.4)	35.2 (35.3)	43.6 (49.2)
Not very/not at all harmful	28.6 (28.3)	47.8 (47.1)	62.3 (62.5)	65.9 (72.1)
Don't know	34.6 (34.2)	24.3 (26.4)	23.8 (24.3)	23.2 (19.3)
Total	100	100	100	100

Score for total population (score for main population group). The question was whether it would be harmful (a threat in the case of Russia) for the country concerned if (after the first NATO expansion round) other East European states (the Baltic States in the case of Russia) would join NATO.
Source: as Table 1.

4. CESDP and ERRF

Where NATO and the EU meet, we find the Common European Security and Defence Policy that has taken off very quickly since 1999. The institutional infrastructure is now in place for a European Rapid Reaction Force (ERRF) to fulfil rescue, peacekeeping and peacemaking tasks from 2003. The (so-called Headline-) goal set in Helsinki calls for 60,000 troops to be deployable within two months and sustainable for up to a year.[9] Will the future member states of the EU – three of them in NATO since 1999 – be able to play a role in the ERRF *before* they accede to the EU? And what will be the role of countries such as Russia and Ukraine? Both future 'insiders' and 'outsiders' have after all given proof of their desire to contribute to European security, not only in diplomatic word, but concretely for example in various forms within KFOR in Kosovo. Recent developments testify to the creativity of diplomatic counter-measures by Russia, Poland, and Ukraine.

In December 1999, in Helsinki, the European Council decided that 'European NATO members who are not EU member states' and 'other countries who are candidates for accession' to the EU 'will be invited to contribute' to the ERRF. This opened the door for countries such as Poland, the Czech Republic, and Hungary. It also said that Russia, Ukraine 'and other interested states' might be invited to take part in EU-led operations.[10] This position was reiterated by the European Council in Portugal, June 2000, and further developed by the Nice Council of December 2000.[11]

So 'how can 'outsiders' be locked into the European security process – barring their membership of NATO or EU? One should note that with this objective in mind, Ukraine and its neighbours to the West have started military co-operation several years ago. In the autumn of 1995 Ukraine and Poland decided to create a joint brigade, which held its first exercises in 1997. A Polish-Ukrainian battalion was later included in the KFOR forces in Kosovo.[12] On this model, in early 1999 the ministers of defence of Ukraine, Romania and Hungary agreed to form a joint battalion under the name Tisza.[13]

The preservation of an independent Ukraine is of great importance to the countries of Central Europe as a guarantee against the revival of Russian dominance.[14] It is welcome to Poland, for example, that Ukraine has been trying to deepen its co-operation with EU and NATO accession states in order to gain a foothold (or bridgehead) in the European integration institutions. To the first Ukrainian President, Kravchuk, Poland served as a 'gateway to the West'.[15] Partly for this reason – some say: also to further the interests of the US – Polish diplomacy has during recent years actively promoted the integration of Ukraine with both the EU and NATO.[16] In this respect it is interesting to note a recent and daring Polish proposal to the EU to include a Ukrainian military battalion in the Polish brigade of around 2,000 troops that (in November 2000) Poland has pledged to serve in the ERRF. On May 15, 2001 Polish Defence Minister Bronislaw Komorowski said in Brussels that Poland had reached agreement on this proposal with the Ukrainian government.[17] As one Polish observer wrote, 'the game for the final structure of the Common Foreign and Security Policy of the EU is not over yet, and it should be exploited in favour of Polish-Ukrainian interests'.[18]

The race for participation in rapid reaction forces is on. A Central Asian one brought into being by Russia with Belarus, Armenia, Kazakhstan, Kyrgizstan and Tajikistan now matches the European force. In Yerevan on May 25, 2001 the presidents of these six countries (participants to the CIS Collective Security Treaty of 1992) signed the founding documents for a joint rapid reaction force of initially 2,000 troops, to be expanded in the future into a larger 'general purpose' force. The force is to be deployed in Central Asia to fight 'Islam fundamentalism' and 'terrorism'. [19]

5. Conclusion

Even though the anti-NATO feelings among the populations of Eastern Europe are limited, further expansion of NATO – to be decided in Prague in November 2002 – will create a backlash in these states and will strengthen their sense of being shut out. Enlargement of the EU is generally considered to provide almost as much of a security guarantee, but will proceed at a slower pace. Continuation of the process of EU enlargement is of great importance both to the future 'insiders' and to the rest of Europe, even though the mutual adaptation is a painful process. It is commendable that the EU has been trying to involve non-member states in the development of its rapid reaction force. But it seems that the role it is reserving for 'permanent outsiders' such as Russia, Belarus, Ukraine, and Moldova will only start after the institutional and military structure of the force has come into being, and after decisions for a concrete intervention have been taken. This will leave the impression with these countries that they are welcome to help clean up messy situations but only *after* the rest of Europe has decided to do so – or worse, has created the mess in the first place. In the interest of a pan-European security, the 'outsider' should be engaged as much as possible. It is therefore so that the recent Polish initiative to include a Ukrainian battalion in its brigade should be dealt with construc-tively, risky as it is.

And finally this. In the countries of Eastern Europe, awareness of the EU and its activities is extremely shallow. Only literally a handful of highly specialised officials in the foreign ministries have any knowledge of the recent, quickly evolving developments in the European security field. And yet it is precisely through the ERRF where Europe, through bold initiatives and flexible diplomacy, might make a difference in firmly tying the 'outsider' states to the future of the continent.

Notes

1   Bovt Georgii. Survey of foreign affairs experts, *Izvestiia* 25 May 2001 as reported in *Johnson's Russia List*, 5268 (25 May 2001).
2   EBRD, *Transition Report 1999: Ten years of transition* (London: EBRD, 1999), p. 73.

3   italics added.

4   Interviews of the 'Outsiders' research team in Chisinau, 18-25 July 2000. See also John Löwenhardt, Ronald J. Hill and Margot Light, 'A wider Europe: the view from Minsk and Chisinau', *International Affairs* (London), 77:3 (July 2001), pp.513-28.

5   The term 'political schizophrenia' was coined by an 'American observer', see Michael Ludwig, 'Partnerschaft im Schatten des Krieges', *Frankfurter Allgemeine Zeitung*, 30 March 1999.

6   *East European Constitutional Review* 9:4, Fall 2000, p. 26.

7   Boratyński Jakub and Gromadzki Grzegorz. *The Half-Open Door: the Eastern Border of the Enlarged European Union* (Warsaw: Stefan Batory Foundation, March 2001. Policy Papers 2), pg. 7. The report contains a catalogue of concrete suggestions for alleviating the impact of 'Schengen' on cross-border movement.

8   For details, see Margot Light, Stephen White and John Löwenhardt, 'A Wider Europe: The view from Moscow and Kyiv, *International Affairs* (London), 76:1 (January 2000), pp. 77-88.

9   For the history of the CESDP and the NATO-EU debate, see Terry Terriff, Mark Webber, Stuart Croft and Jolyon Howorth, 'European Security and Defence Policy After Nice', Briefing Paper, New Series No. 20 (London: Royal Institute of International Affairs, April 2001). Related documents can be found in Maartje Rutten (comp.). *From St-Malo to Nice. European defence: core documents* (Paris: WEU, Institute for Security Studies, May 2001. Chaillot paper 47).

10 See Rutten, *From St-Malo to Nice*, pp. 86, 88.

11 See Rutten, *From St-Malo to Nice*, pp. 124, 174.

12 Wolchuk Roman. 'Ukrainian-Polish Relations Between 1991 and 1998: From the Declarative to the Substantive'. *European Security* 9:1 (Spring 2000), pp.127-56. (p. 142). See also Przemyslaw Zurawski vel Grajewski. 'Polish-Ukrainian Co-operation in the Context of the Future Membership of Poland in the European Union'. CPCFPU Occasional Paper 45 at http://www.foreignpolicy.org.ua/ op/2000ope45.phtml, retrieved 24 May 2001.

13 Zgurets Serhiy. 'Battalion Brotherhood', *The Day* at http://www.day.kiev.ua /DIGEST/1999/4/ daybyday/day-3.htm, retrieved 25 May 2001.

14 Wolchuk, 'Ukrainian-Polish Relations'; Ludwig, 'Partnerschaft im Schatten'.

15 Wolchuk, 'Ukrainian-Polish Relations', p.130.

16 See Missir de Lusignano Alessandro. *Poland's Ostpolitik and EU Accession*. Jean Monnet Lecture, 15 March 2000 at the Centre for Russian and East European Studies, University of Birmingham; and Ludwig, 'Partnerschaft im Schatten'.

17 *RFE/RL Newsline* 5:93 (II), 16 May 2001. Poland had pledged a brigade to the ERRF in November 2000, see *RFE/RL Newsline* 4:227 (II), 22 November 2000.

18 Przemyslaw Zurawski vel Grajewski. 'Polish-Ukrainian Co-operation'.

19 *RFE/RL Newsline* 5:101 (part I), 29 May 2001, and *Monitor*, 30 May 2001.

RUSSIA AND UKRAINE: TOGETHER TO EUROPE?

Lien Verpoest

1. Introduction

Relations between the Russian Federation and the EU are an intriguing issue that has not only been widely discussed in recent years but has also resulted in concrete actions. After the Partnership and Co-operation Agreement, a Common Strategy was issued by the EU, to which the Russian Federation reacted with a Medium-Term Strategy. It could be interesting to expand the discussion of relations between Russia and the European Union and involve Ukraine in the analysis of Russia-EU relations.

In this article I will try to show that one of the 'outsider states' can become an increasingly important factor in relations between the Russian Federation and the European Union. First of all, because Ukraine – together with the Central European states, most of which will soon become EU members – is located between Russia and Western Europe. Moreover, Ukraine has repeatedly been called a 'stabilising factor' on the European continent. Given Ukraine's large population and the considerable surface area that it occupies on the European continent, the European Union has an interest in helping it to become a democratic and politically stable state. Ukraine is important not only geopolitically, but also ideologically. In the future, it could well become a *determining factor* in relations between the European Union and Russia. The question poses itself: who will win Ukraine?

In the first years of independence, Ukraine took a pro-European course. Endeavouring to assert a Ukrainian identity, the country turned its back on Russia and more than once stated its European aspirations. Over the last couple of years, however, Ukraine's situation – and consequently its position – has changed. Ukraine has to an insufficient extent carried out the necessary and expected reforms and the process of democratisation. Economic growth has not been forthcoming. Corruption remains high. The recent scandal (the Gongadze case) plunged the country into a political crisis in which President Leonid Kuchma lost much of his credibility. In short, the European Union (and also the US) is slowly but steadily losing patience. After ten years of independence, it can be concluded that Ukraine's reforms are of substandard performance. The credit that was granted to Ukraine during the transition years is running out. More has to be done, and faster. The recent events in Ukraine have not exactly contributed to the EU's faith in quick changes or solutions. Consequently, this opens up opportunities for Russia. Being a part of Russia's *blizkoe zarubezhe* (near abroad), Ukraine has always been a high foreign policy priority for Russia. On a negative note, one could say that now, more than ever, Russia has an opportunity both to extend its sphere of influence and to strengthen the CIS. Ukraine's continuing – albeit reluctant – membership in the CIS works to the disadvantage of the EU. With the European Union becoming increasingly important on Russia's foreign policy agenda, the question is how Russia will reconcile its positions regarding Ukraine and the EU. Or perhaps Russia sees no need to reconcile the two positions and will conduct a two-track policy. Could this possibly result in new *dividing lines*, a much dreaded term in present day Europe? Will Ukraine become a point of discord for Russia and the European Union, or will it become a uniting factor, leading to co-operation?

This paper is structured as follows. Firstly, a brief overview will be given of Ukraine's development over the last ten years since independence. Secondly, I will touch upon the country's concrete contacts with the West. Thirdly, Ukraine will be situated within Russian foreign policy. By way of conclusion, several possible scenarios or solutions for the future will be suggested.

2. Ukraine: Ten Years of Independence between Russia and the EU

With its 49.9 million inhabitants and 603,700 km² of surface area,[1] Ukraine is one of the largest countries in Europe. The geopolitical position of Ukraine between Western Europe and Russia adds even more importance to the country's situation. Immediately after the collapse of communism, Ukraine was seen by observers as an important test-case for Russian foreign policy. The general opinion was that if Russia declined to acknowledge Ukraine as an independent state, this would demonstrate Russia's intentions to re-incorporate all the former Soviet Republics and to restore its old empire, (an opinion which reflected the typical imperialistic vision of Russia). We can ask ourselves whether this was really the case. If we look at how Ukraine has developed over the last ten years, and how Russia and Europe have taken part in this development, certain tendencies can be distinguished.

a. The Kravchuk years: Identity Formation

In the first years of independence, Russia did not really perceive Ukraine as a serious partner. The Russians found it extremely difficult to come to terms with the existence of an independent Ukraine.[2] Frank Umbach asserts that "in psychological terms, many Russians, including many well-known democrats and liberals of the intelligentsia, have never accepted the sovereignty and independence of Ukraine, a country that has always been 'little Russia' in their eyes. (...) These nationalists repeatedly refer to the historical ties because Ukraine (from the word 'okraina' [sic][3], which means borderland), and especially Kiev, constituted the cultural centre of Russia until the 12th century. In this light, the 'real' Russia still to be established in the near future will be a common Slavic state incorporating at least Ukraine and Belarus".[4]

Another aggravating factor for Ukraine in its relations with Russia was that in addition to – and linked to – the problems of identity formation, there was little or no internal political consensus during the first five years of independence. Opinions were divided between western Ukraine (which, having been part of the Habsburg Empire, had enjoyed somewhat more social freedom and economic development, and where a considerably highly proportion of ethnic Ukrainians reside) and (south)-eastern Ukraine, where more ethnic Russians live (in the Donbas region, Crimea, etc) and which is somewhat more backward economically. Although more than 80% of the Ukrainians voted for independence,[5] differences of opinion surfaced shortly thereafter, a development which in the Crimea region even led to the appearance of separatist movements.

As first president of Ukraine, Leonid Kravchuk rightly focused on the country's problems of national identity and endeavoured to develop a strong national idea. He pursued a policy of Ukrainization. Kravchuk supported national revival, a return to national traditions and the recovery of the historical memories of Ukrainians *and* national minorities.[6] Unfortunately he did not pay much attention to economic reforms.[7] Taras Kuzio stresses in his book on state and nation building in Ukraine that the establishment of statehood and nationhood is impossible without thorough, far-reaching economic reforms. Up until 1996, during this period of national romanticism, the main effort was focused on getting rid of the idea of Ukraine as Russia's little brother.[8] It was during these years of identity formation that a conflict arose between Ukraine and Russia over the division of the Black Sea Fleet.[9] This turned out to be a protracted conflict that strained relations between the two countries for a long time. Normally speaking, after the demise of the Soviet Union and the founding of the Commonwealth of Independent States (CIS), the Black Sea Fleet was supposed to become a part of the CIS armed forces (belonging to the 'strategic forces' division). But Ukraine demanded that half of the fleet, i.e. 200 of the total 400 ships, be put under Ukrainian command. They reckoned that the fleet was on Ukrainian territory. Russia refused, thus igniting the conflict. A series of temporary but inconclusive resolutions followed.

b. Ukraine under President Kuchma: a more pro-Russian Policy?

In 1994, Leonid Danilovich Kuchma won the presidential elections. During the election campaign, he had promoted a much stronger pro-Russian policy than Kravchuk had ever conducted. This stance gained him a lot of support from a broad range of people – even Communists. His pro-Russian attitude probably delivered Kuchma his electoral victory. In 1995, Kuchma reached a provisional agreement on the Black Sea Fleet with president Yeltsin.[10] It provided that the Black Sea Fleet and the facilities belonging to it would be leased by Russia for 20 years.[11] The same year, a friendship treaty was signed by Russia and Ukraine, in which common borders were recognised.[12]

3. Ukraine and the West

Generally speaking, we could conclude from the above that in comparison with the tensions between the two countries that prevailed during the first five years after the collapse of the Soviet Union, there was considerable progress in and amelioration of relations between Russia and Ukraine in the second half of the 90s. Nevertheless, it would be superficial and hasty for us to jump to conclusions of this kind.

It may be that Leonid Kuchma won the presidential elections because of his pro-Russian attitude, but soon after this victory he altered his stance. A change of policy followed, in which his pro-Russian stance was minimised. In 1995, Ukraine became a member of the Council of Europe.[13] In 1997 Ukraine established a 'Distinctive Partnership' with NATO. At that time, Kuchma even declared that NATO was the only organisation in Europe that could guarantee peace.[14] On the whole, Kuchma's shift in policy has exhibited a more European-oriented stance.

The European Union also had interests of its own. Together with Belarus, Ukraine is one of the "outsider states" of the European Union. Nevertheless, the European Union does not fail to attach importance to Ukraine. A Partnership and Co-operation Agreement between Ukraine and the EU was signed on 14 June 1994, and it entered into force in 1998. This Agreement established certain bilateral institutions, such as the Co-operation Council, the Co-operation Committee, and the Parliamentary Co-operation Committee. Ukraine was also the second country (after the Russian Federation) for which the European Union adopted a Common Strategy (at the Helsinki European Council in December 1999). We cannot ignore the fact that Ukraine will become an EU neighbour state after the enlargement. In the Presidency Conclusions of the Göteborg European Council of 15 and 16 June 2001, item 14 elaborates on the co-operation with and importance of Ukraine: "Stable and positive political and economic development in Ukraine is of strategic importance for Europe. The Union acknowledges Ukraine's European aspirations and will continue to support democratic development, human rights, the rule of law and market-oriented economic reforms."[15]

As already mentioned, Ukraine has several times expressed ambitions to join the EU. Minister of Foreign Affairs Anatoly Zlenko stated just recently that "EU integration is not only a strategic goal; it has become an intrinsic factor of state development; it is one of the goals of Ukrainian national development."[16] Although the European Union acknowledges these interests, it does not go further (for instance, with a proposal for associate membership). This is disappointing for Ukraine, but does not hamper its interest in good relations with the EU, which is concretely taking shape in the implementation of an EU-Ukraine Action Plan,[17] with a focus on the twinning of institutions. The Partnership and Co-operation Agreement (PCA, entered into force 1 March 1998) between Ukraine and the EU also includes plans for a Free Trade Area (FTA), though this is preconditioned by WTO membership for Ukraine. Ukraine enjoys EU support in this endeavour, though it is still considered a non-market economy by the EU,[18] so one can wonder just how far Ukraine still is from effectively achieving all these goals.

Ukraine has also institutionalised its relations with NATO. A "Distinctive Partnership between NATO and Ukraine" was signed in Madrid on 9 July 1997. The North Atlantic Council meets approximately twice a year within the framework of the NATO-Ukraine Commission (established by the Charter).[19] Regular consultations are being held; the Political Committee of NATO visited Ukraine three times between 1997 and 2000. Ukrainian troops are also participating within the framework of the NATO-led Stabilisation Force in Bosnia and Herzegovina (SFOR). In January 2001, the Ukrainian government adopted a "State Program for Co-operation of Ukraine with NATO 2001-2004". Further results of this co-operation include an Information Office, a Joint Working Group on Defence Reform, etc.

Marco Carnovale of NATO's Eastern European Partners Section asserted that the NATO-Ukraine Charter of 1997 is not a final stage, but rather a first step in mutual co-operation. Membership is currently not an issue, however. "It is not on our agenda, not on Ukraine's agenda, and it is better this way." On the domestic political crisis in Ukraine, Carnovale commented that "NATO does not want to interfere in the internal affairs of Ukraine, but also has no intention to be indifferent."[20] There is anxiety about how Russia will evaluate the current situation and possibly use it to strengthen its own position in Ukraine.

4. Recent Developments: Scandal and Crisis

The current situation has considerably weakened Ukraine's position. A scandal that surfaced in autumn 2000 resulted in a deep political crisis. Mykola Melnychenko, a former bodyguard of president Kuchma, released tapes[21] containing recordings of conversations of the president and other high government officials, which are meant to prove extensive corruption at high government levels. More importantly, the recordings were also said to contain Kuchma ordering the murder of Georgy Gongadze, the journalist of the (opposition) internet newsletter "Ukrainska Pravda", whose beheaded body was found earlier that year[22] just outside Kiev. The release of the tapes, and the endless discussion and research on whether they were real, sparked a deep crisis in Ukraine. Both the "Ukraine without Kuchma" opposition group and the "National Salvation Front" took shape and there were several demonstrations against the president. They did not succeed, however, in their ultimate objective of forcing the president to step down.[23]

The domestic political situation in Ukraine got even more complicated in February 2001. An alliance between the Communists and the so-called pro-Kuchma (and theoretically pro-governmental) centre and right-of-centre majority in the parliament was formed, which sought to oust Prime Minister Viktor Yushchenko. The unsatisfactory performance of Yushchenko's cabinet in Ukraine's "Reforms for Prosperity" socio-economic programme in 2000 was put forward as the reason for wanting to oust Yushchenko.[24] It should be noted that for the first time since independence, there has been economic growth in Ukraine. Reforms resulted not only in 6 % growth of GDP in 2000, but also the payment of 2.6 billion dollars of commercial debts, the stabilisation of the *hryvna*, a 40% increase in pensions and a 6% increase in real income.[25]

Nevertheless, on April 26, the parliament (*Verkhovna Rada*) voted by 263 to 69 (with 24 abstentions) to approve a resolution accusing Viktor Yushchenko's cabinet of failing to improve the economy and leading the country to ruin.[26]

President Kuchma appointed a new Prime Minister in the end of May: 47-year old Anatoly Kinakh, chairman of the Union of Industrialists and Entrepreneurs. He is a compromise figure ('*kompromissnaya figura*'[27]) who is neutral and is acceptable for all the important fractions in the Ukrainian parliament (except for the Communists and the nationalists).[28] Thus, in a subtle way, Kuchma managed to hush the scandal that almost brought him down and limit the damage resulting from Yushchenko's dismissal by appointing a neutral Prime Minister and reappointing most members of cabinet.

So far the facts. The question now is whether this crisis will influence Ukraine's relations with Russia or with the West.

5. Russia's Foreign Policy: General Evolution

A fundamental problem in the relations between the Russian Federation and Ukraine is that they have divergent views of their foreign policy vis à vis each other. Ukraine wants to conduct an independent foreign policy, whereas Russia sees, for example, the Friendship Treaty of 1997 as a possible means of co-ordinating Ukraine's foreign policy to a certain extent, and ultimately regaining control over it.

Carnovale asserts that even though NATO has special relations and agreements with both Russia and Ukraine, it cannot but see that Russia is tightening the screws on Ukraine, especially in the area of energy. Its debts, in particular, bring Ukraine into a very difficult position vis à vis Russia. Ukraine's gas and energy debts to Russia amount to double the reserves of the National Bank of Ukraine.[29] Over the last decade, Ukraine has regularly obtained extension time for the payment of its debts. As a consequence, Russia has an instrument at its disposal for continuously exerting pressure on Ukraine and thus expanding its sphere of influence.[30] During the political crisis, Putin turned out to be the only head of state who did not criticise Kuchma. Neither did he urge the Ukrainian president to take action and make sure that a transparent investigation into the tapes and the murder of Gongadze would take place. Unlike the European Union, the IMF or the Council of Europe, Putin expressed his support for Kuchma. This is also illustrated by the fact that Russian Federation Council chairman Stroev said that the Russian delegation to the Parliamentary Assembly of the Council of Europe (PACE) will support Ukraine against efforts to suspend or expel it because of Kyiv's media policies.[31]

Is Russia really tightening its grip on Ukraine? Is it true what James Sherr asserts, namely that the Russians have little experience living with neighbours who are both friendly and independent, and therefore are always tending toward (re-)integration? And, moreover, that "many Russians persist in seeing Saint Petersburg as the brain, Moscow as the heart and Kiev as the Mother of Russia"?[32] There are signs that point in this direction.

One can say with certainty that Russian foreign policy – or better, the *approach towards* Russian foreign policy – has altered since Vladimir Putin became president of the Russian Federation. President Putin has disciplined the multi-voiced confusion of Russian foreign policy.[33] One of the main traits and criticisms of Russian foreign policy is the lack of a consistent stance or vision.[34] Different policymakers advocated divergent visions, which was (to say the least) rather confusing. Several different foreign policy concepts were drafted in the early nineties, but never thoroughly developed. Nonetheless, certain features of the policies of the different ministers of foreign affairs can be distinguished. After the romantic period of Kozyrev followed (in 1996) the 'selfish Realpolitik' of Evgeny Primakov.[35] Official documents, however, which could shed more light on the Russian government's position on foreign policy, were lacking. During the year 2000 (Vladimir Putin was elected president on 26 March 2000), there was a sudden boom in the publication of official documents. On

10 January 2000, the *Kontseptsiya Natsional'noy Bezopasnosti Rossiyskoy Federatsii* (National Security Concept of the Russian Federation) appeared. In April, a *Voennaya Doktrina Rossiiskoy Federatsii* (Military Doctrine of the Russian Federation) followed. In October 2000, the *Kontseptsiya Vneshney Politiki Rossiyskoy Federatsii* (Foreign Policy Concept of the Russian Federation) was published.[36] However, the fact that a lot of texts were suddenly released by the Ministry of Foreign Affairs is not necessarily a sign of a radical shift in foreign policy, as much as it might be a sign of a *general* change originating in Putin's arrival.

A careful reading of the Foreign Policy Concept of the Russian Federation reveals certain formulations that show a relative continuity of foreign policy in the successive governments. It states that "the Russian Federation is pursuing an independent and constructive foreign policy. It is based on consistency and predictability, on *mutually advantageous pragmatism.*"[37] Russia sees itself as a (regional) superpower, and aims to restore this status and perception in the rest of the world. This stance does not really differ from Primakov's foreign policy concept. Tom Casier summarises Primakov's foreign policy model as follows: "The *objective* is to restore Russia's position as a great power. The *means* to reach this objective is to consistently observe Russia's national interests. The *worldview* underlying the objective is that of a multipolar world."[38] Putin shares this view.

Yet there are some shifts of accent in the new Foreign Policy Concept. For instance, Russia is now clearly focusing on Europe, whereas during the Primakov era this focus was perhaps not so apparent. Back then, good relations with the United States were preponderant. In the Foreign Policy Concept, there is mention of the threat of evolving towards a unipolar world (dominated by America). Other than that, America is left more or less on the sideline in the text. More attention goes to establishing good relations with Europe, which is called "Russia's traditional foreign policy priority"[39] in the text. The best illustration of this is the Medium Term Strategy of the Russian Federation towards the European Union (2000-2010), which was published in October 2000. In this text as well, Russia profiles itself as a great power and a strategic partner of Europe. Of course this focus on Europe originates in Russia's pragmatism. At the current time, it is simply more advantageous to establish good relations with the European Union, especially in view of the economic perspectives. The EU is Russia's largest trading partner, accounting for 36.7% of its imports and 33.2% of its export trade. Hence, *pragmatism* remains one of the principal and continuing features of Russian Foreign Policy, be it under Primakov or Ivanov. From the political perspective, as well, there is the pragmatism of endeavouring to counterweigh the unipolar threat of the U.S. With the government of Putin, a different, perhaps more 'professional' or 'modern' *approach*[40] to conducting foreign policy has been initiated, though the objectives and general traits remain roughly the same.

6. Russian Foreign Policy Towards the Near Abroad

Does the same apply to Russia's foreign policy towards its close foreign neighbours, including Ukraine?

Even though Russia defines itself as a superpower and although its main objective is to become one again, for the moment Russia is more of a major regional power. As already mentioned, Russia has had difficulties seeing Ukraine as a separate entity and an independent state. From a Russian point of view, Ukraine, Belarus and Russia form the indivisible Slavic Core of the Commonwealth of Independent States. Ukraine and Belarus are not only considered to be the same people (Eastern Slavs), but the relations between Ukraine, Belarus and the Russian Federation are being situated within the institutional structure of the CIS. For Belarus, and more specifically for Alyaksandr Lukashenko, this is not a problem at all. During the visit of the Patriarch of Moscow and All Russia, Aleksey II, on 27 June 2001, Lukashenko in his typical way "urged the fraternal peoples of the three Slavic states to unite".[41] Belarus is eager for closer co-operation with Russia because this would imply more financial support within the framework of the Russia-Belarus union.

Ukraine, however, has always been reluctant about deeper integration into the CIS.[42] But the current political crisis and the enormous debts of Ukraine to Russia do not put Ukraine in a position to refuse further integration. For these reasons, Ukraine has no other choice than to co-operate with Russia. Leonid Kuchma himself gives yet another reason: "Both Ukraine and Europe are consuming Russian gas, without which we cannot manage. This also includes Russian oil and other Russian raw resources. Moreover, Russia is a market for Ukrainian products. Are we allowed into Europe with our products? Europe is closed for us. So, if we left Russia, where would we go?" He adds: "Ukraine should have good relations with Russia for the sake of regional security and for the sake of general stability on the European continent. All of us are interested in a stable Russia – all of us without exception, including Europe".[43]

It is exactly *regional security* that is one of the main focal points of the Russian Federation's foreign policy. Due to major changes in the international situation, such as the eastward expansion of NATO, the Kosovo crisis and EU enlargement, as well as the recent statements of President George Bush on NMD, Russia feels under political pressure. Because of all these recent developments, there is fear of geopolitical isolation. Therefore, James Sherr asserts,

Russia has no choice but to transform the ex-USSR into a security zone. He adds that it will not be a case of re-integration, but rather of re-subordination[44].

As one can read in the Foreign Policy Concept of the Russian Federation, "a priority area in Russia's foreign policy is ensuring conformity of multilateral and bilateral cooperation with the member states of the Commonwealth of Independent States (CIS) to national security tasks of the country".[45] The expression 'ensuring conformity' does not necessarily mean re-subordination. It could imply that Russia is reasserting its leading role in the CIS area. During the CIS – summit in June 2001, is was remarkable to see Russia conducting a great deal of bilateral negotiations on the sidelines of the summit, and sometimes acting as an intermediary for two other member states. The spokesman at the press conference, moreover, was the Russian Minister of Foreign Affairs, Ivanov, who spoke in the name of the CIS.

Nevertheless, for the specific case of Ukraine, it can be said that Russia has intensified its 'conformity' efforts. There are signs of institutional changes in Ukraine, based on the Russian model. In early June, 2001, there were reports of Ukraine carrying out military reforms based on the model of the Russian military (namely, reducing the armed forces, as is being done in the Russian Federation).[46] Economically, as well, Russia is increasing pressure. H. Van Zon notes that Russia plans to completely eliminate Ukraine in the energy sector. "The Russian government is negotiating an agreement to build a pipeline to Turkey under the Black Sea and to build a pipeline through Belarus and Poland, bypassing Ukraine. This means that eventually the Russians will be able to do without the Ukrainian pipeline, thus making it easier to cut off the energy supplies to Ukraine altogether". Another recent event, the appointment of ex-prime minister and Gazprom mogul Viktor Chernomyrdin as the new Russian ambassador in Kiev cannot but be interpreted as a further increase of Russian influence on Ukraine.[47]

It is an undeniable fact that the Russian Federation is pulling Ukraine closer, but one can ask in which way. Although many Russians endlessly reiterate the close cultural and historical links between the two countries, we would be jumping to conclusions if we called Russia's stance neo-imperialistic. At least there is no explicit,[48] confrontational *political* imperialism. In my opinion, Russia is currently (re)acting in conformity with its foreign policy concept, which is characterised by pragmatism and the intention to promote 'mutually advantageous cooperation'. It is unfortunate that the United States[49] – and especially the European Union – have had to exert so much pressure on Ukraine due to the recent crisis. It is especially unfortunate because the European Union was already putting intense economic pressure and imposing high expectations on Ukraine even before the crisis occurred. This fact added to Ukraine's disappointment and discontent with the EU, practically driving the country into the arms of Russia.[50]

In this situation, the important difference between Ukrainian *nezalezhnost* (formal independence) and *samostiynost* (which also means independence, but with the connotation of 'the ability to stand on your own feet') is becoming painfully apparent. It is a simple fact that as long as Ukraine has energy debts with Russia, and as long as there are no serious economic reforms (which seemed to have taken off under Yushchenko), it will be impossible to deepen the relations with the West that could eventually form a counterweight to the economic dependence upon Russia.[51]

In this way, unfortunately, the Russian foreign policy of 'mutually advanta-geous co-operation' is advantageous for Russia because it pulls the strings, and for Ukraine only because there is no other alternative at the current time. The least that can be said is that Russia's foreign policy should be reformulated in terms of the situation of 'dependence' that actually exists, rather than in terms of 'co-operation' or 'interdependence'. In the case of Ukraine, 'mutually advantageous co-operation' appears to be a hollow concept.

7. Possible Scenarios for the Future

How will relations between Russia, Europe and Ukraine develop in the future? There are different possible scenarios. First of all, as long as Ukraine does not manage to carry out the much-needed reforms, the only possible scenario will be that of Russia increasing its economic – and possibly also political – influence, and attempting to incorporate Ukraine into its sphere of influence under the pretext of strengthening CIS structure.

A second scenario would be a rapprochement between Ukraine and the EU and a deepening and further development of relations with the United States, but this scenario does not seem very likely for the moment. As democratic states, the countries of the European Union and the United States cannot tolerate the level of corruption and the scandals in Ukraine. Ukraine was recently ranked the third most corrupt country in the world by the civil society (anti-graft) organisation Transparency International.[52] America's credibility will be damaged if it continues to provide financial support to such a country when no serious changes in economic policy are being implemented by the Ukrainian government and when there are no signs of any movement towards true democracy, development and the tolerance of civil society. The European Union does not underestimate the geopolitical importance of Ukraine. There is an awareness that the enlarged Union will share borders with Ukraine. The EU wants to avoid a situation in which Ukraine would feel itself to be an outsider state. Several channels of co-operation have been opened since Ukrainian independence (e.g. within the framework of the Common Strategy and TACIS).[53] Both America and the EU are worried that Ukraine might become "a Russian puppet",[54] a possibility which they have attempted to avoid by taking a number of different actions through a number of different channels over the past decade. I think, however, that there is insufficient awareness of how this process is taking place at the current time and how it has been significantly intensified since the crisis and the ouster of Viktor Yushchenko. The only possible way to avoid it is for the US and the EU to make a radical shift in foreign policy, but such a shift is for the time being not feasible.

Thirdly, would it be on the other hand such a disaster if the Russian Federation were to draw Ukraine closer to itself? Hans Van Zon comments that a revived Russian sphere of influence and Ukrainian submission therein would not constitute a military security threat for the EU in the conventional sense. The economic base of Russia will be too weak in the short and medium term to support a significant military build-up. Hence the question is not so much whether Ukraine will or will not develop close relations with Russia, but whether de-stabilisation in the regions of the former Soviet Union will destabilise other parts of Europe. "A 'Slavic Unity' scenario would not be the worst if it would lead to political stability in the region".[55] Numerous policies and the general political culture of the Ukrainian government show more affinity with Russia than they do with Europe. Democratisation has not been fully completed, and perhaps we must simply admit that, as for now, Ukrainian institutions and political culture are more in tune with Russia and Eastern Europe than they are with Western Europe.

For this reason, it can also be interesting to mention a fourth possible option or scenario. In theories of international relations, all of what has been described above can be subsumed under the older theory of realism. In contemporary debates on International Relations, Ukraine is always immediately linked to Russia, or at least the future relations with Russia are extensively discussed (and, according to some, over-emphasised).[56] More recently, there has also been a greatly increased focus on Ukraine's relations with Europe. Nonetheless, the role which Central Europe can play in this area is often underrated.

Realist thinking mostly encompasses reasoning about 'security dilemmas' and 'balance of power'. However, global-level changes such as the collapse of the Soviet Union and the resulting downfall of communism totally altered the international political scene. Suddenly, new Central and Eastern European states emerged, the Russian Federation took over the seat of the Soviet Union in some international organisations but turned out to be a weakened superpower, ... and so on. All these events of the past decade have changed the very nature of international relations. Hence it is logical that the thinking on International

Relations should be adjusted to these new conditions as well. Margarita Balmaceda cites two important new issues: the importance of *institutions* and of *alliances*.

The emphasis on institutions is an idea advocated mainly by 'neo-liberal institutionalists'. They argue that institutions moderate the international environment by creating automatic security obligations of a collective character. Neo-realists like John Mearsheimer argue the opposite: that institutions cannot have an independent effect on state behaviour. According to them, the behaviour of states is determined by power realities, and an unjustified faith in the ability of institutions to foster peace can be very dangerous, as it may bind states and statesmen to the realities of aggression.[57] Still, for Ukraine, regional institutions are important. Since Ukraine must do without NATO and EU membership, it would be an important step towards further co-operation and the development of Ukraine's (above-mentioned) 'balancing' position (especially now that this position could change into bandwagoning) if the country were to become a member of institutions such as CEFTA[58] and if it were to become more involved in transborder initiatives such as the Carpathian Euroregion. Mearsheimer argues that effective institution building is much easier to achieve in the economic field than in the security field.[59] This certainly applies to Ukraine. Ukraine's military weight is too significant and the pressure from Russia would become too great. These regional institutions and economic co-operation are therefore a good alternative.[60]

The candidate countries of the Visegrad group could well play an intermediary role between the European Union and Ukraine. But this is a more or less ideal picture of how things could be since the reality is that Russia is the dominant power in the region. The Central European States might escape the Russian sphere of influence by applying for EU and NATO –membership,[61] but Ukraine does not have this option for the time being. The Russian Federation will not allow such a thing to happen for a country that is part of the Slavic core of the Commonwealth of Independent States.

And, finally, there is the importance of alliances. "The question of whether a new 'bipolar' order will emerge in the region – that is, an expanded NATO up to Ukraine's western borders, and a Russia-led military alliance including Belarus and pressuring Ukraine to join – will be crucial for both Ukraine and Central Europe."[62] Even though Taras Kuzio claims that external threats have been overestimated by the Ukrainian government which, in his view, has always over-concentrated on them,[63] the importance of alliance patterns is emerging and increasing. Whereas within the paradigm of realism, alliance patterns were mainly viewed in military terms, now alliances can be perceived in other ways as well. Stephen Walt brings up the ideas of *balancing* and *bandwagoning*.[64] "Bandwagoning refers to a situation in which states seek to align with the source of danger or the dominant power in the region; Balancing refers to a situation in which states seek allies in order to create a balance against a prevailing threat."[65] In the case of Ukraine, since Ukrainian independence, this balancing seems to have been more likely – and a better option – than bandwagoning. Since 1992 it has been the intention of the Ukrainian government to play a balancing role in alliance formation in the area. Within this framework, Ukraine's policy of 'Neutrality, Non-Nuclear and Non-Block Status', officially proclaimed in 1993, could be seen not so much as a 'real' declaration of neutrality, but as primarily a means of balancing a Russian-dominated CIS with new foreign-policy initiatives directed at other Central European States and the West.

In the light of the current circumstances, this could change. Due to its weakened position and the fact that (because of NATO enlargement) Russia is seeking to expand its zone of regional security, Ukraine might be forced to go for the 'bandwagoning' option (in the sense of 'aligning with the source of danger or the dominant power in the region'). Russia does not perceive this in such a negative light as Ukraine does. It formulates the bandwagoning option in a more eloquent way: "Rossiya i Ukraina: v Evropu – vmeste", meaning "Russia and Ukraine – moving together towards Europe". Sergey Markov (Director of the Institute for Political Research) perceives the relations between Russia and Ukraine as follows: *"[For Ukraine,] Integration with the CIS is impossible: this organisation is becoming a 'president's club'. Integration through the union of Russia and Belarus is also hardly possible: Ukraine is too different from Belarus in many respects. Ukraine cannot become a EU member on its own: the Europeans are only giving obscure promises that are worth nothing. There are also no possibilities of central European integration since all central European states have decided to join the EU separately. Therefore, the most realistic option is to co-operate with Russia in a joint attempt to become EU members – 'Moving together towards Europe'. This formula clearly expresses a common desire for European integration. It is obvious that Russia and Ukraine will have different roles and conditions, but the goal of internal Europeanisation should be common to both."*[66]

It is of course striking how differently Russia perceives its relations with Ukraine than vice versa. Nevertheless, for now the most pragmatic solution might be for Ukraine to take the bandwagoning option and in this way secure its position. Better to move together towards Europe than not to move at all towards Europe.

Notes

1 For a short overview of Ukraine (and its relations with the EU), see http://europa.eu.int/comm/external_relations/ukraine/intro/index.htm

2   Aleksandrova O. Die Aussenpolitik der Ukraine nach dem Machtswechsel. *Berichte des Bundesinstituts für ostwissenschaftliche und internationale Studien*, 3-1996, 34.

3   David Saunders writes: "[the Ukrainians] described themselves as *rusyny*, a term which merely indicated descent from the inhabitants of the medieval principality of Rus'. The ethnic term 'Ukrainian', though not the geographical expression 'the Ukraine' (or 'Ukraine'), is a late-nineteenth-century invention which was adopted by most of the people to whom it applies only after 1917." In: Saunders, D. *Russia in the Age of Reaction and Reform 1801-1881.* London/NY, Longman, 1994, 180.

4   Umbach F. Russia and the Problems of Ukraine's Cohesion: Results of a Fact-Finding Mission. *Berichte des Bundesinstituts für ostwissenschaftliche und internationale Studien*, 13-1994. That Russia could not really accept the idea of Ukraine, the 'borderland', as a separate country, was also reflected in the fact that Russian diplomats and senior advisers warned the Eastern European countries not to develop too close ties with Ukraine, because it fell within Russia's sphere of influence and its independence would be a temporary phenomenon only. They added that Ukrainian embassies soon would be downgraded to consular sections. Of course, this kind of attitude caused serious frictions between the two countries. In: "You'd be nervous living next to a Bear" in *The Economist*, 15-5-1993. Especially Zhirinovsky could not wait till Russia would re-annex Ukraine.

5   Wanner C. *Burden of Dreams: History and Identity in Post-Soviet Ukraine.* Pennsylvania, Pennsylvania State University Press, 1998.

6   Kuzio T. *Ukraine. State and Nation Building.* London, Routledge, 1998, 22.

7   Leonid Kuchma, on the other hand, did not underestimate the importance of stable economic and social conditions. He was quoted as saying "Genuine statehood is impossible without a stable, well-developed economy, social well-being and dignified living condition for the citizens." In: *Ukrainian Weekly*, 22 December 1996.

8   Saunders D. *Russia in the Age of Reaction and Reform 1801-1881.*London/NY, Longman, 1994, 179-181. For a good overview of Ukraine's history and its historical ties with Russia, see Lieven A. *Ukraine and Russia. A Fraternal Rivalry.* Washington D.C., United States Institute of Peace Press, 1999, p 11-49 (with timeline).

9   The conflict started in February 1992.

10 In 1997, a final agreement was signed.

11 One could wonder here what state the ships and equipment of the Black Sea Fleet will be in at that time. Already now, the vessels are seriously out of date.

12 On 18 January 2001, Russian defense minister Igor Sergeev met with his Ukrainian counterpart Oleksander Kuzmuk. They signed a cooperation plan that includes 52 projects, amongst others the creation of a joint command

post in Sevastopol and a joint rescue detachment of the Black Sea Fleet. In: RFE/RL Newsline Vol. 5, No. 13, Part II, 19/01/2001.

13 Although recently, the Council of Europe was deliberating on whether to bar membership due to the recent crisis. See: *The Europeans*, Parliamentary Assembly of the Council of Europe News Bulletin, April 2001, Issue 26: "The Assembly's Monitoring Committee believes that Ukraine has failed to fully honor the obligations and commitments it made when joining the organisation in 1995. In a draft recommendation adopted at its last meeting, the committee recommends that the Committee of Ministers take the statutory steps to exclude Ukraine from membership of the Council of Europe. The committee regretted that in spite of its previous resolutions the Ukrainian authorities have not adopted new laws on human rights protection and legal reform."

14 Garnett S. *Keystone in the Arch: Ukraine in the Emerging Security Environment of Central and Eastern Europe.* Carnegie Endowment for International Peace, 1997.

15 Göteborg European Council: Presidency Conclusions. 15/06/2001, No. 200/01.

16 Minister of Foreign Affairs Anatoly Zlenko, as quoted in his speech during the International Conference "The EU and Ukraine", Brussels, 24/01/2001.

17 http://europa.eu.int/comm/external_relations/ceeca/tacis/ap2000_ukraine.pdf.

18 "Joint Statement by President Chirac and Javier Solana and President Kuchma in Conclusion of the EU-Ukraine Summit on 15 September 2000." In the Press Release it was announced that the "EU Council is considering removing Ukraine from the list of non-market economies in the EC antidumping legislation and granting it the same treatment as Russia and China in antidumping proceedings." Hence, up to that time, Ukraine was still considered that way. http://europa.eu.int/comm/external_relations/ukraine/intro/summit_15_09_00.htm

19 The NATO-Ukraine Commission met for the first time in Kiev in March 2000.

20 Marco Carnovale, as quoted in his speech during the International TEPSA Conference "The EU and Ukraine", Brussels, 24/01/2001.

21 Melnychenko did this via Oleksander Moroz, leader of the Ukrainian socialist party. Moroz handed over the tapes to the prosecutor general. Later on, the tapes were examined by different authorities and agencies, including the FBI. Melnychenko obtained refugee status in the United States. Recently he was said to have gained special witness status, after handing over audio recordings to the US authorities suggesting that 1 billion dollars has been deposited in US bank accounts that either belong to or are controlled by Leonid Kuchma. In RFE/RL(Un)Civil Societies, Vol. 2, No. 24, 13/06/2001.

22 The decapitated body of Gongadze was confirmed to be found on 16 November 2000, two months after he disappeared in September): RFE/RL Newsline Vol. 4, No. 223, Part II, 16/11/2000.

23 Not only the Ukrainian people, but also the international community expressed concern about the events in Ukraine. A triumvirate of Foreign and Security Policy Commissioner Javier Solana, Swedish Foreign Minister Anna Lindh (Sweden was at that time President of the European Union) and External Relations Commissioner Chris Patten visited Ukraine in February and warned the Ukrainian government to maintain a free press and a transparent policy. Several countries and organisations urged Kuchma and the Ukrainian government to take action and to make sure the Gongadze – case was being thoroughly investigated. At a certain moment, the Council of Europe even threatened to cancel Ukraine's membership.

24 RFE/RL NEWSLINE Vol. 5, No. 41, Part II, 28/2/2001.

25 RFE/RL Poland, Belarus, and Ukraine Report, Vol. 3, No. 16, 1 May 2001.

26 Zasidannya tridtsat' vos'me: Sesiyniy zal Verkhovnoi Radi Ukraini. 26 kvitnya 2001 roku. 10.00 godina, pitannya nr. 7235, 7235-1, 7235-2. Apart from the Communist Party caucus, the motion was supported by lawmakers from the Labor Ukraine, Social Democratic Party (United), Democratic Union, Ukraine's Regions, Greens, Popular Democratic Party, and Yabluko parliamentary groups. "*Uryad vipravleno u vistavku.*" Ukrain'ska Pravda, 26/04/2001.

27 Timoshenko V. "Segodnya Ukraina poluchit novogo prem'era?" – *Nezavisimaya Gazeta*, 24/05/2001. An interesting thought raised in this article is that the person of Kinakh can be compared to Evgeniy Primakov. Both became Prime Minister in a time that the president (then in Russia Yeltsin, now in Ukraine Kuchma) needed a compromise figure to get on better terms with the Parliament.

28 His (rather unnoticed) previous political career illustrates his compromise-profile: he was deputy minister under Evgeny Marchuk (1995), was elected MEP in 1998 (under Lazarenko), and was reintroduced into government in 1999 under prime minister Valeriy Pustovoytenko as deputy minister for industrial policy. Kinakh managed to live in peace with all three prime ministers. Ivzhenko T. "Ocherednoy 'Chelovek Prezidenta'?" – *Nezavisimaya Gazeta*, 29/05/2001.

29 John Tedstrom, former White House adviser on Ukraine and Russia, quoted from a speech given on 26 April 2001 at the University of Leuven.

30 With the West, the (economic) relations recently have slightly improved. After the IMF cancelled its loans, Ukraine nevertheless managed to pay off a part of the debts. More importantly, for the first time since independence, the Ukrainian economy made progress. Also for next year, a growth of 6-7% is predicted. Many ascribe this economic progress to (now ex-) prime minister Viktor Yushchenko.

31 RFE/RL Newsline Vol. 5, No. 81, Part I, 26 April 2001

32 James Sherr, (Lincoln College, Oxford University / Conflict Study Research Center of the Ministry of Defense), quoted from his speech on the International TEPSA conference "The EU and Ukraine", 24/04/2001.

33 James Sherr, (Lincoln College, Oxford University / Conflict Study Research Center of the Ministry of Defense), quoted from his speech on the International TEPSA conference "The EU and Ukraine", 24/04/2001.

34 Trofimenko H. *Russian National Interests and the Current Crisis in Russia.* London, Ashgate, 1999.

35 Casier Tom. *The Evolution of Russia's Foreign policy and the concept of National Interest,* paper for the VI ICCEES World Congress, Tampere, 2000, p 1.

36 The foreign policy concept of the Russian Federation was approved by President Putin on 28 June 2000. Since September 2000, several other documents have been released by the Russian Ministry of Foreign Affairs: "Doktrina Informatsionnoy Bezopasnosti" on 9/9/2000, and "Kontseptsiya Prigranichnogo Sotrudnichestva v Rossiyskoy Federatsii" on 13/02/2001.

37 *The Foreign Policy Concept of the Russian Federation.* Approved by the President of the Russian Federation Vladimir Putin. June 28, 2000. http://www.mid.ru/mid/eng/econcept.htm

38 Casier Tom. *The Evolution of Russia's Foreign policy and the concept of National Interest,* paper for the VI ICCEES World Congress, Tampere, 2000, p 2.

39 The Foreign Policy Concept of the Russian Federation. Approved by the President of the Russian Federation, Vladimir Putin. 28 June 2000, p.8. http://www.mid.ru/mid/eng/econcept.htm

40 For example, trying to obtain (an impression of) transparency by publishing official documents on the MFA website, as well as speeches of Minister Ivanov and daily news briefings.

41 "Alexey II and Alexander Lukashenko urge the peoples of Russia, Belarus and Ukraine to unite", Russian Observer, 27/06/2001. (www.russianobserver.com)

42 Ukraine's position concerning its place in the Commonwealth of Independent States (CIS) caused only more tensions. Right from the very start of the CIS, Ukraine never favoured a deep integration into CIS -structures. Olga Alexandrova sums up the Ukrainian policy towards the CIS (in 1996): "Ukraine wants a special status within the framework of the CIS. It refuses to enter those specific CIS-structures which, from the Russian vantage point, are most important to re-integration. The extent of Ukraine's participation in the structures of the CIS must not be incompatible with the country's constitution, with it declaration of sovereignty, with its declaration of independence, or with Ukrainian laws. National interests and the country's security take priority; Preservation of sovereignty, opposition to all attempts to impose supra-state structures on the CIS; No state is permitted to dominate the inter-state organisations; No all-embracing "re-integration",

but gradual, evolutionary integration solely in the economic field; The evolution of relations with the states of the CIS must not interfere with Ukraine's relations with the leading industrial nations. In: Aleksandrova O. Die Aussenpolitik der Ukraine nach dem Machtswechsel. *Berichte des Bundesinstituts für ostwissenschaftliche und internationale Studien*, 3-1996, 35.

43 Interview with President Leonid Kuchma, On the relations between Ukraine and Russia. *RFE/RL Poland, Belarus, and Ukraine Report*, Vol. 3, No. 14, 17 March 2001

44 James Sherr (Lincoln College, Oxford University / Conflict Study Research Center of the Ministry of Defense), quoted from his speech on the conference "The EU and Ukraine", 24/04/2001.

45 The Foreign Policy Concept of the Russian Federation. Approved by the President of the Russian Federation Vladimir Putin.. June 28, 2000, p.7. http://www.mid.ru/mid/eng/econcept.htm

46 Georgiev V. "Ukrainskaya voennaya reforma po rossiyskomu obraztsu". In: *Nezavisimaya Gazeta*, 01/06/2001. Ukraine plans to reduce its armed forces by one third. The author of the article draws a parallel between Russia and Ukraine, claiming that "…like Russia, Ukraine is trying to carry out military reforms, but under even more difficult circumstances, originating in a permanent economic crisis, energy resources shortage, and insufficient development of the military-industrial structure for weapons production." (my translation)

47 Viktor Chernomyrdin was appointed by President Putin on 10 May 2001. See: Timoshenko V. "Moskva naznachila v Kiev namestnika" – *Nezavisimaya Gazeta*, 11/05/2001.

48 On the other hand, implicitly Russia does exert political pressure on Ukraine.

49 The US has been put in a difficult position since they gave the Ukraine so much financial support and now is compromised by the murder case and the corruption scandals in the very country to which they gave such financial support. See Karatnycky A. "Meltdown in Ukraine. To Russia with Love?" – *Foreign Affairs*, May/June 2001, Issue 3, p 73. Motivated by the strategic importance of this country of 50 million people and worried that it might become a Russian puppet, the U.S. government provided $2.8 billion in aid to encourage democratic reform. These funds were supplemented by additional billions from western Europe and substantial loans from the International Monetary Fund and the World Bank." and Monaghan E. "Ex-Bodyguard calls Kuchma tapes real". – *The Moscow Times*, 27/06/2001, p.8.

50 According to James Sherr, this increasing pressure from the EU is driving a wedge between Ukraine and the EU.

51 See also Van Zon H. *The Relations of the European Union with Ukraine. A very difficult Partnership*. Proceedings of the International TEPSA Conference "The EU and Ukraine", April 2001, 16.

52 See www.transparency.org, 2001 Corruption Perceptions Index (CPI), survey carried out in collaboration–with the University of Göttingen.

53 See Ukraine's TACIS Indicative and Action Programmes, http://europa. eu.int/comm/external_relations/ceeca/tacis/ind_act_prog.htm

54 Karatnycky A. "Meltdown in Ukraine. To Russia with Love?" – *Foreign Affairs*, May/June 2001, Issue 3, p 74.

55 Van Zon H. *The Relations of the European Union with Ukraine. A very difficult Partnership*. Proceedings of the International TEPSA Conference "The EU and Ukraine" April 2001, 16.

56 Balmaceda M.M. (ed.) *On the Edge. Ukrainian-Central European* – Russian Security Triangle. Budapest, Central European Press, 2000, 17.

57 Mearsheimer J. 'The False Promise of International Institutions', *International Security* 19, No. 3, (winter 1994/1995), 49.

58 Or also, a closer cooperation with the countries of the Visegrad group.

59 Mearsheimer J. 'The False Promise of International Institutions', *International Security* 19, No. 3, (winter 1994/1995), 49.

60 Ukraine could join CEFTA around 2005 if it fulfils the necessary conditions. See: Balmaceda M.M. (ed.) *On the Edge. Ukrainian-Central European – Russian Security Triangle*. Budapest, Central European Press, 2000, 255.

61 Although there is still the tricky case of NATO-membership for the Baltic States.

62 Balmaceda M.M. (ed.) On the Edge. Ukrainian-Central European – Russian Security Triangle. Budapest, Central European Press, 2000, 19.

63 Kuzio T. *Ukrainian Security Policy*. Washington: Praeger, 1995, 49.

64 Walt S. *The Origins of Alliances*. NYC, Ithaca, Cornell University Press, 1987, p.17. see also Balmaceda M.M. (ed.) On the Edge. Ukrainian-Central European – Russian Security Triangle. Budapest, Central European Press, 2000, 16-23.

65 Walt S. *The Origins of Alliances*. NYC, Ithaca, Cornell University Press, 1987, p.19. Walt asserts that weak states have the propensity to bandwagon.

66 Markov S. "V Evropu – vmeste. Novyy etap v otnosheniyakh Rossii i Ukrainy". – *Nezavisimaya Gazeta*, 29-08-2001. English translation: Moving Toward Europe Together http://www.therussianissues.com

Russian Security Policy and Developing EU-Russia Relationships in the Political and Security Field

Dmitry Danilov

1. Introduction

The end of the Cold War has opened up a broad perspective in Europe not only for East-West rapprochement, but also for the construction of a common Wider Europe based on the idea of pan-European co-operation. However attractive the concept of building the 'Common European home' was in the past, it remained just a general ideal which was far removed from practical European policies. Undoubtedly, Gorbachev's 'Common European home' euphoria was perceptible in the West as well, particularly during the fall of the Berlin Wall and of the Velvet Revolutions in Central and Eastern Europe. But in the West this euphoria was overcome very quickly and replaced by a pragmatic Western approach.

Eastern Europe, or the post-Soviet space, has become an area of high instability, where the forces of disintegration have been aggravated by political crises, ethno-political conflicts and increased social and economic tensions. The direct military threat from the East has been replaced by a new and serious challenge of instability in the post-Soviet arena. Uniting with such an unstable East can in any event not be considered a suitable Western response to the security challenge. This would only spread the destructive consequences of Eastern instability all around Europe. Precisely these realities, rather than a lack of political will – for which the West often was and is blamed in Russia – have set the objective limitations for the development of the pan-European process.

In this situation the West has deliberately concentrated its efforts on the adjustment and reinforcement of its own institutions, while at the same time developing an infrastructure for political dialogue and for careful, limited co-operation with its Eastern neighbours. Facing the danger of communist revenge in the East, or a restoration of the old confrontations, and seeking to strive against the negative developments in the post-Soviet space, the West declared its readiness to develop a pan-European partnership. However, this promising rhetoric appears to be essentially the wrapping of a Western practical policy.

Russia has largely retreated from its illusory perception of the Western stance, attempting to push the West into what is frequently termed a 'strategic' partnership. As a consequence, Russia's Western and European policy proved increasingly ineffective and reactive. The lack of active policy and its rather ideological nature boosted the extremely dangerous tendency towards isolation or self-isolation of Russia in Europe and in the world. This was confirmed by severe defeats of key points of Russian external policy in recent years.

Russia counted on the political will and common sense of the West, unsuccessfully trying to convince it: (1) not to enlarge NATO eastwards; (2) not to undertake military operations in Yugoslavia without UN Security Council authorisation; (3) not to adopt the strategy of projecting NATO's military force out-of-area; (4) not to oppose the construction of the European security system with the OSCE on top of an institutional pyramid; (5) not to try to restrain the Russian activities in Chechnya. But, paradoxically, international events and tendencies, unfavourable for Russia in its relations with the West, induced Russia to revise its perception of international relations, leading to a more pragmatic approach and to a conceptual reappraisal of its place and role in Europe and the world as a whole. In this context, for example, notwithstanding the defeat of Russian diplomacy in the Balkans in 1999, under this shock therapy Russian policy was given an incentive to reassess its security relations with the West, and to do so not in a confrontational, but in a pragmatic manner.

Undoubtedly, Russia could regret that it failed to defend its concept of collective security at the Istanbul OSCE Summit in November 1999. But a result in the opposite direction seemed to be more important: Russia was successful in withdrawing its unrealistic concept, driving it into isolation among its partners in the OSCE. Documented in the Istanbul Charter, the rejection 'to create an hierarchy of the organisations or to establish a permanent division of labour between them' did not bury the all-European processes. On the contrary, with these decisions, the new prospects for constructive co-operation of interlocking European security institutions were open without precondition to OSCE's 'key and uniting role' in Europe.

A pragmatic approach also manifested itself in Russia-NATO relations, which became distinctly less frosty in March 2000. Russia dropped its reluctance to co-operate with NATO and demonstrated an openness towards a constructive relationship. However, it pointed out that the content of this co-operation would be highly dependent on how NATO responds to Russia's main concerns and, first of all, on the confirmation by NATO of key principles and obligations which from the Russian point of view had been violated by the Alliance (Foreign Policy Concept). The Russian National Security Concept includes NATO enlargement in the list of military threats, posing the danger of destabilisation of the strategic situation as a result of unilateral power actions by the Alliance. NATO enlargement is described as one of the major threats to international relations. It is linked to two other threats which are prioritised by the Concept – undermining the role of the UN and OSCE and the 'threat of a decline in Russia's political, economic and military influence in the world'. The military threat is determined as 'NATO's shift, confirmed in its strategic doctrine, to the exercise of power (military) actions out-of-area of the Alliance and without the authorisation of the UN Security Council'.

However, given that the option of establishing a Russia-NATO strategic partnership is likely to be very marginal for the near future (even if it is not ruled out by both parties in principle), and in the light of the current anti-NATO mood in Russian public opinion and among the elite, it should be recognised that the real scope for co-operation between Russia and NATO is rather limited. One possible way of accommodating a relative deficit in the Russian-Western security relationship would be to intensify the European channels – EU/WEU as well as bilateral relations between Russia and leading Western countries.

The problem of the political self-identification of Russia is essentially reduced to the historic choice between its integration in Europe and its separation from the rest of Europe. Non-European choices for Russia – any alternative geo-strategic orientation or isolationism – are not considered to be a viable response to the long-term Russian priorities and/or to be realistic. Taking into account an acceleration in European integration and in the development of Euro-Atlantic co-operation, the redrawing of the European map, the external dependence of Russia and the decline in its international influence, the task of developing Russia's long-term foreign policy and security strategy is acutely evident.

In this context, one of the main tasks is undoubtedly to define the Russian position vis-à-vis the European Union's common foreign policy, especially in its security and defence dimension. Russia must take the following issues into account: firstly, the importance of the EU as a preferential partner for Russia; secondly, a relatively new but dynamic process of formation of ESDP; thirdly, a Russia striving to improve its security relations with the West; and fourthly, increasing in particular the international policy and security dialogue and interaction with its European partners.

There is much detail in the Russian attitude towards ESDP and the EU-Russia co-operation in the security and defence matters that shows, on the one hand, the general constants and roots of the Russian policy in this direction, and on the other hand its changes under President Vladimir Putin. An overview could provide a better understanding of the prospects for political and security relations between Russia and the European Union.

2. A 'European Legacy' for President Putin

In recent years Russia has confirmed its intention of developing a special relationship with Western Europe in its foreign policy, including co-operation in security matters. This is in line with the Russian foreign policy principle of 'equal approach'. The general motives are quite obvious. After the Cold War, objective possibilities for progressively developing Russian-European political relations as well as mutual interests emerged. Distinct 'American' accents in Russian foreign policy were gradually removed. As a result, a positive motivation for more active co-operation between Russia and Europe increased both at bilateral and institutional level. However, bilateral relations with the leading European states turned out to be more beneficial for Moscow. Although the postponement of the coming into force of the PCA until December 1997 was a contributory factor, the main reason was the objective insufficiency of the EU's CFSP as well as of the WEU's potential, augmented by Russian scepticism with regard to prospective common European security and, in particular, defence possibilities.

The institutionalisation of the Russia-EU relationship, as a result of the PCA coming into force and the strengthening of the EU's 'second pillar' due to the Amsterdam Treaty, contributed to increasing possibilities of political and security co-operation between the two sides. At the very first session of the Co-operation Council in January 1998, Evgeny Primakov (then Russian Minister of Foreign Affairs) appealed for practical co-operation in resolving international problems. Such an interest remained vital in the Russian approach under Vladimir Putin. Vassily Likhachev, the Russian Permanent Representative to the European Communities, worded it as follows: 'The main aim in the RF-EU dialogue is to replace the policy of information exchange with co-ordinated decisions and actions. Prerequisites for such behaviour of both parties exist. It is important to introduce them into international practice.'

At the same time, another motive for Moscow was the hope that relations with Western Europe could be used as an additional lever to influence the US and NATO, which continued to be more important focuses of Russian security policy. Addressing Western Europe, Russia reacted against (in Russian eyes) negative tendencies in NATO's policies, particularly enlargement and the unauthorised use of out-of-area force. Aleksandr Avdeev, the Russian First Deputy Minister of Foreign Affairs recognised in late 1998 that: 'The military-political component in our dialogue with the EU is still mainly attached to the transformation of the North Atlantic Alliance, revision of its strategic concept, in particular its approach to peace-keeping'.

Such a combination of two opposing motives for developing relations with Western Europe – let us call them the positive and the non-constructive ones

– considerably limited the real, rather than declaratory, potential for co-operation. Firstly, the non-constructive motives made it impossible for Russia to concentrate its political energy on constructive security co-operation in fields of genuine common interest. Secondly, the understanding by Europe of the 'hidden' rationale of Russian interests meant it felt unable to rely on Russia as a significant and consistent partner. Thirdly, in this situation a closer political and security relationship between Russia and the EU would be perceived negatively by other countries, namely the US and the Central and Eastern European States.

But despite the existence of such non-constructive Russian motives, it should be recognised that they were never predominant. It is particularly important to note that the core objective has not been to oppose Europe against America or its other partners. Instead, recently it has been Russia's positive aspiration to bring Russian and European interests closer to each other and to co-operate on that basis. Russia looked forward to being better understood by Western European counterparts in a situation where understanding with others had become more problematic. Consequently, Russia demonstrated its willingness to support the positive dynamics in political relations with Western Europe even under circumstances of political crisis with NATO and aggravation of the relations with the US.

In this sense the newly elected President Putin began his term of office with a mainly positive 'European' legacy. However, insufficient clarity of Russia's 'European' policy in the Yeltsin period, contradictions in its motives and aims, conceptual and institutional fragmentation of the decision-making process – including in the security sphere – made the question about the future of that legacy acute. Its acuteness was particularly conditioned, firstly, by the urgency for the new Russian leadership to elaborate its programme for the country's development (to strengthen foreign and security policy), and secondly, by a considerably changed international situation in which this had to be done. The shaping of Putin's European policy was influenced by some relatively new and contradictory factors resulting from events in Kosovo and Chechnya, and changes in the policies of the US, NATO, EU/WEU as well as in their relations with Russia.

The Kosovo Crisis

On the one hand, doubts about the ability of Western Europe to conduct an independent policy have been increasing in Russia. At the same time, the Yugoslav events and NATO's new Strategic Concept have made it obvious that European interests, formulated in the context of NATO policy, differed from Russian interests. On the other hand, one of the political implications of the Kosovo crisis was the increasing inducement to ESDP. For Russia in this situation time was needed to see the correlation of these opposing vectors in the European security and defence co-operation and their impact on the short-term practical policy of the EU.

Kosovo has provoked a crisis in NATO-Russia relations due to differences of principle in the parties' approaches to some crucial problems for Russia. It is quite obvious that these problems cannot be resolved in a short time, and this limits the scope for Russia-NATO co-operation. This became a motive for a reappraisal by Russia of the experience of and prospects for its security relations with the West, and increased the arguments to make Russia's 'European' policy more active.

First of all, this activation of Russia's European policy was pre-conditioned by the need to hold out against dragging the negative tendencies of relations with NATO into the whole Russian-Western relationship. Secondly, Russia cannot allow itself to remain indifferent towards Europe given the importance of co-operation with Europe for promoting domestic development and progress in reforms. Thirdly, taking into account the relative vacuum in the Russian-Western security relationship, there was an objective Russian interest in finding additional opportunities for dialogue. Fourthly, Russia considered the peacekeeping potential of NATO, which remained an effective military machine and was mainly focused on military-power actions, to be functionally limited and inadequate to meet the manifest challenges in European security.

Therefore, the EU with its developing ESDP dimension was seen as a potentially more appropriate institution and partner, focused on a broader, multifunctional security approach, including peace-keeping and crisis management.

The 'Chechnya Factor'

The Chechnya factor has undoubtedly limited the prospects for EU-Russian political and security co-operation. After the EU Summit in Helsinki in December 1999, it was first of all a matter of restoring the relationship, which had deteriorated. This took precedence over new steps and initiatives towards the development of interaction in the security sphere, which was intrinsically very delicate and problematic. Both parties were simply forced to take a pause. The question was how long it would continue and whether 'Chechnya' would be the main obstacle to developing EU-Russian political and security co-operation. This question became especially acute under the French Presidency of the EU because of the particularly tough attitude taken by France to Russian actions in Chechnya.

Secondly, the insertion of the Chechen issues into the EU-Russia dialogue showed clearly that the increase in its flexibility and effectiveness (as it was accepted before Chechnya, by the EU-Russia Summit in October 1999) presumes that Russia has to agree to discuss with the EU some crucial aspects of internal policy. The new Russian leadership agreed, and as a result the Chechen question did not become the main issue in EU-Russia relations and its acuteness has gradually diminished.

The EU Common Strategy towards Russia

The EU Common Strategy towards Russia was perceived by Moscow as a very positive signal from the EU, especially taking into account that the Strategy was adopted in June 1999, in a climate of growing disputes between Russia and the West on Kosovo-related issues. In addition, this Strategy was the first document of its kind, giving priority to relations between the EU and a third country, namely Russia. Without going into the details of the Strategy, it undoubtedly opened up a new perspective and these initiatives in fact became a kind of European message to Vladimir Putin, who took up the position of Acting President in January 2000.

Even before January 2000, the Common Strategy and the political relations with the EU became a focus of special attention for Vladimir Putin, because he (and not Boris Yeltsin) presented the 'Russian response' – the Medium-Term Strategy for the development of relations between the Russian Federation and the EU at the Helsinki Summit of October 1999.

Thus, both documents laid the foundations for EU-Russian political and security relations and became a point for particular attention for the new Russian leadership.

Nevertheless, the Russian medium-term Strategy looks less promising in comparison with the EU document. It never clearly answered the question of Moscow's attitude towards accelerating CFSP and the establishment of ESDP with its military dimension. According to this document, the partnership with the EU means support by Russia of the EU efforts in areas, which are important for the Union and where both parties' interests coincide. For example, it was not indicated whether the EU's efforts towards ESDP were relevant, and the Strategy only provided for elaboration in the future of the Russian position towards the 'defence identity' of the EU absorbing the WEU.

In fact, this Strategy refocused the new Russian leadership towards the problem of basic decisions on serious challenges. The transition of the EU/WEU into a new quality force of unity and ability in the security and defence sphere is also a relatively new factor influencing Russian policy. Today's Russian leadership has to proceed from this new situation, differing in principle from the 'Yeltsin period', taking into account that the question of whether or not the EU will have its own defence and security dimension, has been decided definitively. The basic components of ESDP are under active construction and will be available within two or three years. The uncertainty regarding the development of the EU/WEU in the field of foreign policy, security and defence changed in nature, and now applies only to concrete modalities of the practical construction of ESDP.

In this connection, overcoming a reactive character and working out a more definite Russian attitude and strategy became the main tasks for Russian policy in this direction as well.

In order to elaborate this policy, key attention must to be paid to an evaluation of the potential effectiveness of ESDP, as well as the extent of the EU's autonomy in resolving European security problems.

It is a matter of special importance to take into consideration two kinds of exaggeration in the public debate in Russia (and the EU). One is an excessive accent on the EU's shortcomings and on its dependence on the US in the security field. The other, on the contrary, is the exaggeration of the EU's developing security and defence potential, enabling it to be a strong and relatively independent player in international security in the near future.

If Moscow accepts the first extreme, for example, it would be reluctant regarding the development of direct international and security policy links with the EU. Acceptance of the second extreme, on the other hand, would consider the EU as a possible substitute for NATO and the US in Europe as well as in Russian policy. As usual, a middle course, at which Russia should aim in working out its foreign and security policy, seems to be the most realistic option.

3. Potential EU Autonomy in the Security and Defence Sphere

First of all, it must be clearly understood that ESDP will not absorb the functions of collective defence. Even if the extremely difficult decision to abolish the WEU definitively as an organisation is taken and consequently the Brussels Treaty's Article V on mutual guarantees is included in any form into the EU's legal basis (for example as a special protocol amending the Treaty on European Union), then it will still be NATO that provides for collective defence. It is quite clear that the mutual guarantees provided under Article V, even if shaped within the EU, could not be achieved in practice without the creation of European allied military forces with integrated command structures, including proper European nuclear forces, which should be able to respond adequately to the potential danger of a large-scale military conflict in Europe. However, this is not only off the current EU agenda of defence co-operation, but also cannot be considered in many respects to be a real prospective of the EU and ESDP in the foreseeable future.

In this respect, the option of an EU collective defence could be possible in the future if the EU member states (or some of them) were united in a European system of mutual political guarantees and consultations. This implies, however, that in the event of aggression the EU will resort to other, institutionally non-European operational assets and capabilities – those of NATO. This optional development of the EU would probably resemble the initial period of the Atlantic Alliance, which was mainly a 'paper treaty' until the early 1950s when it developed into a fully fledged Organisation (NATO) with permanent political and military structures.

Taking into account this natural structural shortage of the EU, two conclusions can be drawn, which are of major significance for the elaboration of the Russian attitude towards common European security and defence. Firstly, there are neither any intentions nor any real foundations for the creation of some kind of European army in addition to or as a substitution for the existing allied military structures. Secondly, there are also no grounds for an erosion of NATO's principal function of collective defence and, consequently, of the indispensable role of the US.

Therefore, in spite of the intention set out in the Treaty on European Union eventually to create a common defence system, ESDP is aimed at tasks apart from Article V: at withstanding challenges and threats which are not related to the collective defence of the member states. In any case, when developing ESDP, the EU clearly implies that its general goal is to position itself as an autonomous political player, to safeguard the EU's vital interests not only in Europe, but also in its relations with other powers. In this connection, the EU's developing capacities in crisis management are of great significance, not so much as a value in itself, but rather as an important instrument in achieving this strategic goal. A problem could arise with the prospective European ability to deal with crisis management if the United States should move away from its direct involvement in resolving these crises.

All this affirms that the main criteria of ESDP effectiveness will relate to an extent to which the EU should be able to display its *political* identity in the international security sphere, not excluding co-operation with its partners. In other words, the question is how extensive and reliable the operational potential and instruments at the disposal of the EU will be to assume greater responsibility and autonomy in the European security system.

For the short term the EU will apparently have the capacity to conduct only low-scale Petersberg operations. Firstly, its crisis management capabilities will in any case be insufficient to carry out the Kosovo-type operations, while this is considered to be its goal when developing European rapid reaction forces. Secondly, maintaining and consolidating the American role in Europe is hardly compatible with the eventual US refusal to take part in regulation of the serious crisis situations there.

Taking this into consideration, Europeans will be able to assign their new operational capabilities and mechanisms to the Petersberg tasks of relatively lower intensity and complexity. In this respect, two principal operational options exist. The first is the carrying out by the EU of entirely autonomous operations, geared to a limited range of tasks and with limited capability. The second possibility is to conduct more complex European operations, in which the EU's operational deficiency could be compensated by putting NATO's assets at the EU's disposal.

The first operational model places the European Union in a certain peacekeeping 'niche', while under the second option one could hardly speak of real EU autonomy. EU access to NATO resources and assets will not be automatic but rather on a case-by-case basis, as became clear after the North Atlantic Council in December 2000 due to Turkey's opposition. It means that EU decisions on the content and mandate of such a European operation will depend on consensus in the NATO Council in each concrete case. In addition, using NATO's assets in fact means putting American military capabilities, compensating for European deficiencies, under EU command. Could this be imagined in practice without US political control? Even if this were the case, it is unclear why Americans should not want to do the same through NATO. Consequently, if European crisis management responsibility and involvement should arise, it is more a matter of a new division of responsibility in the Transatlantic Alliance, not of political and strategic autonomy.

In two years' time, when the European rapid reaction forces and the crisis management mechanisms are to be created, the EU will primarily be faced with the task of assessing and demonstrating the credibility of its capabilities. At the same time, a similar task should be put on the agenda within the framework of the completion in 2004 of NATO's concept of Combined Joint Task Forces (CJTF). This should open up the practical possibility of using the Alliance's resources and assets in European operations. But cynically speaking, although EU, NATO and the US would be interested in a successful demonstration of European capacity, it will be very difficult to find an appropriate operation for the EU.

Europeans would be interested in carrying out a serious independent Petersberg mission, because a relatively simple one would not prove the EU's new ability. But this does not correspond to the EU's own capabilities or to US and NATO motivations. Taking into account that the EU could conduct a wholly independent operation merely in the lower Petersberg spectrum, NATO and the US seem to be interested assigning a higher-level crisis management operation to the EU in order to link it to the CJTF. However, even if such a possibility were to be found in Europe, it could only underline the lasting dependence of the EU. Moreover, in the event of European operational failure, it could discredit ESDP and perhaps to some extent the CJTF as well.

The optimum choice in such circumstances would probably be a non-European theatre for a European operation, for example in Africa. It was precisely these possibilities that UN Secretary General Kofi Annan envisaged during his talks with EU leaders about the development of co-operation in peacekeeping between the two organisations. Such an out-of-Europe operation would bring the opportunity, on the one hand, for the full-scale application of the EU's anti-crisis potential, whilst still allowing for the use – should it be considered necessary – of NATO assets. This would offer a great deal of European autonomy, bearing in mind that the US would not be politically engaged. Another possibility would be to establish a horizontal division of labour between the EU and NATO, each being charged with different missions within the framework of a common peacekeeping action.

The general conclusion from this analysis of the EU's operational capabilities in the field of crisis management is that it will be relatively limited in the short and medium term. At the same time, however, certain factors could favour an increase in Europe's role and autonomy.

Firstly, the EU will be focused on carrying out operations of mainly fairly low level and intensity. This in turn will result in an increase in EU activity in preventive policy and actions, including police and military actions. The EU has already begun to move in this direction. Javier Solana, Secretary-General of the EU Council, and Chris Patten, Commissioner for External Relations, presented to the Nice Council in December 2000 their joint report on the EU's activities in the field of conflict prevention. The report emphasises that the EU has to 'shift from a culture of reaction to a culture of prevention' and proposes a series of concrete measures for the short and long term. In this connection Solana and Patten argue that the EU 'is well placed to engage in conflict prevention', as it has instruments ranging from trade policy to co-operation agreements, from development assistance to policies on social and environmental matters, from humanitarian aid to civilian and military crisis management capabilities, from diplomatic instruments to co-operation in the area of Justice and Home Affairs.

And this leads us to the second factor of the prospective rise of the EU's role and voice in the international security system.

Secondly, the European Union will aim to develop and implement a complex anti-crisis policy, which should combine a large spectrum of resources and instruments – economic, financial, political and military. In this respect, the EU's position and potential are really unique.

Thirdly, non-military anti-crisis activities could become an important EU specialisation. To give just one example, the European Union could in the near future become the only international organisation having at its disposal a multinational police force, established and trained specifically to operate in crisis and conflict situations. Recent peacekeeping actions have demonstrated clearly critical deficiency of and need for this element of crisis management. Therefore, the EU's role in international peacekeeping activity is clearly set to grow.

To what extent will these factors contribute to an increase in the political and security role of the European Union, in spite of its relatively limited autonomous capacity in crisis management? This will largely depend on developments in the European security situation. There are sufficient grounds for expecting the further emergence and escalation of ethno-political conflicts in Europe. This would objectively lead to the use of massive military force in the framework of peace-making or peace-enforcement. However, such a possibility is hardly probable after the fall of the Milosevic regime.

All countries of Southern, Eastern and Central Europe are without exception involved in a developing process of integration into Euro-Atlantic structures. These countries consider this co-operative inclusiveness and integration as their inevitable development strategy. This is undoubtedly a long-term stabilising factor in Europe, but there are also increasing possibilities for the European powers and institutions to keep the situation in these regions under control. It should also be borne in mind that almost all conflict areas in these regions are also under international control, and the realisation of peacekeeping programmes is continuing there. The aggravation of the situation on the border between Kosovo and Macedonia owing to military actions by Albanian nationalists illustrates that although the former Yugoslav territory remains a zone of tension, this is not a matter of Kosovo-type proportions.

Consequently, in this new European situation the relatively limited operational potential of the European Union should be commensurate with the practical tasks which it will face within the reality of the European integration area. NATO's potential to conduct large-scale peace-making and peace-enforcement operations will be the 'insurance' policy in the event of the emergence of such challenges. At the same time, the EU should seize the opportunity to gradually increase its own capabilities, extending the range of operational missions which it could accomplish autonomously.

When evaluating the outputs of the new EU dynamics in the security and defence field, therefore, and particularly when elaborating the Russian approach, the main conclusion is as follows: in spite of the fact that the creation of EU operational capabilities to carry out Petersberg operations will be relatively limited in the short and medium term, at the same time those capabilities could make a considerable contribution to increasing the role and responsibility of the EU in resolving European security problems.

This new political reality, resulting from the increase in EU security and defence capacity and the concomitant growth in its stature in international politics, face the Union's partners with the task of defining their attitude and strategy towards these developments.

The US has managed to elaborate its strategy and this in turn is an indispensable factor in ESDP development. In general, the US supports the increasing EU security and defence responsibility while emphasising that this process is wholly included into the context of Atlantic solidarity and must increase the cohesion of the Alliance. As an insurance against any European revision of transatlantic relations, the US holds to the formula of the three 'Ds', which must be excluded when developing the EU's ESDP and NATO's ESDI: they are *Duplication, Discrimination* and *Decoupling*. For NATO's part, Lord Robertson stated the need to ensure that ESDI will be based on three 'Is': *Improvement* (in European defence capabilities), *Inclusiveness* (and transparency for all Allies) and *Indivisibility* (of transatlantic security, based on shared values). The definition of the Russian interests towards EU security and defence co-operation is a matter of urgency not only for Russia itself, but also for its European partners concerned about Russian reactions and policy.

4. Prospects for Russian-EU Political and Security Relations

In 2000 a package of new conceptual documents was adopted in Russia – the National Security Concept, Foreign Policy Concept and the Military Doctrine, which can be considered as the programme of the new Putin leadership. They confirm the increasing European accents in Russian policy. According to the Foreign Policy Concept, Russia has the aim of strategic partnership, in addition to the EU, only with CIS states. President Putin, for his part, has repeatedly and insistently emphasised the European choice of Russia, the course towards the strategic partnership with the European Union.

The core of the Russian position vis-à-vis the EU is the acceptance of European integration, including EU enlargement, as a crucial stabilisation factor for Europe in general. This approach excludes a negative attitude by Moscow towards ESDP, which is one of the most important elements in EU integration strategy. But at the same time, the Russian Medium-Term Strategy, as well as three new conceptual documents, retains an open choice between two options: a neutral interest towards ESDP or a positively constructive approach.

In the context of the first relationship model, Russia and the EU would develop their security relations to the extent that ESDP potential and EU political independence increase. The second option assumes that Russia would contribute to ESDP development in order to strengthen its potential. The partners (both the EU and Russia) would accordingly co-ordinate their policy and undertake common actions in the sphere of European security. In this case, ESDP would represent a very important dimension of an EU-Russian 'joint venture', aimed at strengthening European security and at the construction of a Wider Europe.

The results of the EU-Russia Summit in May 2000 demonstrated that Russia could move towards the second, active option. For the first time it was stated in a common declaration that: 'President Putin has expressed a positive interest towards framing European security and defence policy' and has mentioned existing co-operation possibilities. But even after this Summit, the Russian foreign policy establishment has been sceptical regarding the possibilities for putting forward certain new Russian initiatives on ESDP. There was a degree of political inertia hindering new approaches, as well as two additional factors. First was the desire to wait for the decisions of the EU Nice Summit on crisis management co-operation with third parties. Secondly, it was difficult for Russia to initiate new proposals during the French Presidency of the EU due to the latter's special position with regard to Chechnya as well as to general difficulties in Russian-French bilateral relations.

But a different view also existed, which argued that Russia should not waste time and must adopt a more active stance towards co-operation with the EU regarding foreign policy, security and defence matters. This viewpoint (corresponding to the second option) gradually came to predominate in the Russian Ministry of Foreign Affairs, particularly on the eve of the EU-Russia Summit in Paris in October 2000.

There are reasons for believing that a breakthrough in EU-Russian political and security relations was made at the Paris Summit. In principle, their new quality is determined by the transition from declaratory rhetoric to concrete steps. The Russian attitude towards ESDP took the form of constructive support. The common decision was taken to establish special EU-Russian consultations on security and defence matters. There was also a move away from the declaratory 'examining the possibilities' for Russian participation in Petersberg operations towards concrete 'examination of the modalities for Russian contribution'. All this should increase the significance and add to the substance of the dialogue, as well as to its participants' responsibility for the outcomes.

The latter should have a special impact on the Russian side, given that up to the Paris Summit ESDP was not a matter for serious attention for Russian official bodies. Even in the Ministry of Foreign Affairs, to which these functions were attributed, the ESDP issue was of secondary importance at best. ESDP was not a matter for other bodies such as the Security Council, Ministry of Defence, General Staff, or State Duma. Now, the officially adopted task of making EU-Russian security and defence co-operation concrete and practicable should reverse this situation. The Security Council staff has already shown interest regarding these issues, and the military authorities have decided to look into the matter of Russian-EU security and defence co-operation.

There is no adequate expertise on ESDP in Russia, notably in the framework of the decision-making structure. This causes potential difficulties in implementing the leadership's policy decisions. At the same time, there are many complications regarding the relative uncertainty of ESDP, and primarily its institutional problems. The question of the 'due level' and modalities of Russian-European consultations remains unclear. The existing EU institutional components may be used in different combinations (the EU Troika, the Council General Secretariat, the Presidency, the European Commission), and these different options will influence the content and perspective of EU-Russian security co-operation. There are also questions about the parliamentary dimension, notably regarding the option of future joint crisis management; about the parties' direct military-to-military co-operation and participation of the military officials in mutual consultation mechanisms; and about information exchange and protection. There are also more fundamental problems, concerning, for example, the defence industry and trade. This list could be added to, particularly given that practical security and defence co-operation between the EU and Russia is only beginning. However, such problems are already on the agenda of the EU-Russian dialogue, and this in itself is evidence of the transition of the EU-Russian political and security relationship to a new dimension, to a new stage of active, practical co-operation. The question of the need for mutual political and security co-operation was answered positively by both parties. Consequently, they are going to answer other questions: how far forward would they be prepared to move and which ways and means would be most appropriate.

RUSSIA: OUTSIDE EUROPE?

Vladimir Ronin

Russia and *Europe*, how do the two concepts relate to one another? Does Russia historically, culturally and psychologically belong to Europe or does it belong somewhere in between Europe and Asia? Whole libraries could be filled with the texts that have been written on this issue. It is an endless discussion that is ideologically charged, especially for Russians. Everyone knows that it is not merely a geographical matter. Russia and Europe are both complex cultural-historical concepts whose contents have changed several times in the 20ᵗʰ century. For most people, both Russia and Europe symbolise certain social and political values. The Russian State still bears the historical burden of its authoritarian and imperialist traditions, while contemporary Europe is associated with modern democracy.

1. Two Complex Concepts

Does Russia belong to Europe or not? This is in no way a neutral, purely academic question. Many answers are dictated by politics. A Russian who places Russia closer to Western and Central Europe in his analysis, inevitably presents himself as a pro-Western liberal. But authors who place Russia as far outside Europe as possible also have clearly defined political intentions: they want a *particular road* for Russia, they want an isolationist and authoritarian state and a permanent confrontation with the West. Those who cannot identify with European modernity like to talk about Russia as *Eurasia*; they like to stress the need for an *Asian* orientation, towards Iran and China for instance.

After more than half a century of Iron Curtain and Cold War, there is a great deal of terminological confusion on both sides of our continent. Geography requires everyone to consider Russia as part of Europe, but in no other context can we find such certainty. In Russia, the phrases *We and the Europeans* and *We as Europeans* are used interchangeably. In international contacts, Russians as well as their foreign partners may include Russia in Europe on one occasion but not on the next, quite arbitrarily and always depending on someone's concrete intentions and interests. In the mass consciousness of the people in Western Europe, the term *Europe* is still often limited to the European Union, in which not only Russia is excluded, but also the future member states in Central Europe. And in case people in the West do not exclude Poland, the Czech Republic and the other countries of the former Warsaw Pact, they use the term *Eastern Europe* instead of *Central Europe*. While geography may refer to the

Ural Mountains as the eastern border of Europe, in most political and cultural discourse, the CIS-countries and especially Russia are still placed outside Europe.

Is it possible then to achieve more clarity and objectivity on the Russia/Europe issue? Some fundamental acts about some European features of Russia can be summed up, and certain sensitivities that the Russians have with regard to Europe can be explained. There are three levels at which the Russia/Europe issue can be discussed: (1) at the level of the various ideas that Russian philosophers and writers have been airing on the issue for more than 200 years now, (2) at the level of the facts and figures, and (3) at the level of the spontaneous sentiments of the Russian people. The picture at the level of the ideas is very contradictory and the fact that these contradictory ideas are often quoted in the Russian mass media adds to the lack of clarity. If we only listen to what Russians *say*, we will not get a clear answer to the question whether Russia belongs in Europe or not. There is a great deal of uncertainty and the various political tenors contradict one another. If we look at the facts and figures, however, i.e. at the historical, cultural and psychological development of the Russian society, we can clearly see a dominating *European* tendency. And, last but not least, the spontaneous sentiments, inclinations and phobias of Russians often say a great deal about where they place themselves.

Sometimes it is necessary to take a closer look at even the most well known geographical and historical facts to dispel certain myths. What experts on Russia regard as a truism may contain valuable new information for a lay audience in the West.

2. Geography

27% of Russia's territory is geographically located in Europe and 73% in Asia. Does this mean that Russia is 73% Asian? Geographically it is; demographically, however, it is the other way round. The vast majority of the population lives in the European part of the country, to the west of the Ural Mountains. What Russians refer to as Central Russia is located in the European part, roughly speaking between the Volga River, the Dniepr and the lower reaches of the Don. This is the historical core of Russia, its cultural and psychological centre, its heart. What the Russians consider typically Russian – in the landscape and in the climate, in the language and in the national traditions – bears reference to this large region around Moscow, which actually lies on the western edge of the country.

Of even greater importance is the fact that the Asian part of Russia is not a completely different cultural and psychological unit, clearly separated from European Russia by the Urals. In the mass consciousness of the people of

Western Europe, as well as in many Western geopolitical statements, there is something like a Ural myth: people imagine a high and steep wall, which concludes Europe in the East. In the West people often talk about *Russia* and *Siberia*, as if they were two separate entities, lying next to one another and divided by the Ural Mountains.

In fact, the Urals, which are quite old but not very high, are not a border nor a real dividing line. The mountains have never been a barrier for Russian expansion to the east. It is true that Siberia historically developed as a colony, as some kind of supplement and that for Russians it was psychologically isolated to some extent until well into the 20th century. But in the meantime, both objectively and in the eyes of the Russians, Siberia has become an organic part of Russia, just like the Volga region or the area around the town of St Petersburg. Siberia is an organic and natural continuation of Central Russia to the east. The Asian part has been colonised for centuries by people from extremely diverse areas of Russia and the Ukraine, making it a linguistic and cultural mixture and a continuation of the *old country* in Europe, a continuation of the truly European *motherland*.

In the 20th century, Russia has experienced so many internal migrations (normal economic migrations, forced large-scale migrations under the communist regime for major construction projects such as canals, railway lines, dams, and of course migrations because of the evacuation during the war and the Stalinist mass deportations) that almost the same mixture of traditions has developed all over the country. Thanks to the enormous communist centralisation and the enforced uniformity of the Russian language and culture, there are hardly any local dialects or cultural variations among ethnic Russians (more than 80% of the total population) today. Russia is linguistically, culturally and psychologically one space, from the Baltic Sea to the Pacific Ocean. It is true, the country has 12 large regions, spread over 9 time-zones, and is, according to the current constitution, a federation of 89 autonomous territories, but there is no bipartite Russia, no dualism between the European and Asian parts.

The Russians on both sides of the Urals recognise one another as being Russian, albeit only in a general sense. This feeling is both cultural-historical and political, and relates mostly to the Russian State. The Russian view on their country is often strongly state-oriented. For its inhabitants, Russia's history is that of the Russian State and begins with the dynasty of Rurik. Their patriotism is first of all based on the idea of a superpower and on the recollection of military victories. No matter how proud the Russians are of their great literature, art and science, it is above all the thousand-year-old Russian State on which their national identity is based. Wherever the Russian State is present, the same feeling of 'We are one nation' prevails among the Russians, whether it be in Moscow, Kaliningrad, Novosibirsk or Vladivostok.

Of course, the enormous distances within Russia influence the sense of togetherness of the Russians. People in Moscow or in St Petersburg say *Over there, behind the Urals*, and they have the feeling that Siberia is very far away. On the other hand, in the outlying areas of the country people say that *Moscow is very far away*. In North Siberia or in the Far East they talk about *materik – the motherland, the mainland*, by which they mean all regions of Russia where it is less cold and easier to live. Of course, there is also a regional patriotism in the sense of *We along the Volga* or *We in the Altai region*. But no Russian would ever think of claiming that there is another Russia somewhere, where other Russians live. On the contrary, Russians feel Russian in the same way, no matter where they are. They belong to the same Russia, to the same state, to the same linguistic and cultural community, and they have the same mentality. The purely geographical division between European Russia and Asian Russia is of no relevance in this.

The fact that the immeasurable space between the Baltic Sea and the Pacific Ocean is an indivisible unit, is an important fact in itself, also in politics. Whatever the answer is to the question *Does Russia belong to Europe or not?*, the answer goes for the whole of Russia. Even theoretically, the country cannot be divided into two parts and the Ural Mountains are not a border. If Russia is included in Europe, this Greater Europe does not stop at the Urals, but extends all the way to the Pacific. If from a historical, cultural and psychological point of view one considers Moscow and St Petersburg to be European, one has to consider modern Siberia as European as well. Europe stretching all the way to the Pacific Ocean? The indivisibility of Russia is both a problem and a challenge for the European integration in general. Even if we stick to the Gaullistic formula *to the Urals*, Russian membership is not immediately evident in all European structures. Such a formal integration of the indivisible Russia extending to the Far East is totally unthinkable from a purely geometric point of view. However, in the long term, an immense continuum between the Atlantic and the Pacific Ocean which sees itself as Europe, could present a colossal opportunity for the liberal and democratic values in the world and of course for the political and economic position of a united Europe.

Russian history clearly demonstrates how large the opening to Central and Western Europe always has been. We are not necessarily talking about Western influences, but more about common elements or a certain parallelism in the historic development of Russia on the one hand, and what people have traditionally referred to as Europe on the other. The European orientation of Russian history rests on two fundamental factors. Firstly, we see that Russia and most of the countries of Europe share a common Christian heritage (knowledge, ideas, cultural inspiration, social and moral values, etc.); secondly, we see that the cultural exchange between Russia and Central and Western Europe has been uninterrupted for over 1,100 years.

3. History and Culture

During the first 350 years of its history, between the 9th and the 13th century (the period of Kievan Rus), the Old Russia bore many similarities in its social and political structures to countries such as Poland and the Czech lands. As in all early medieval countries outside the Roman Empire, Old Russian society was dominated by the power of government, while the rights of individuals developed very slowly. This is not a Western European model, but it is not exclusively Russian either. It is just one of the European models of that time. In many fields, the rulers of Kiev had very intensive contacts with the whole of Europe. The three daughters of Prince Yaroslav the Wise marrying the Kings of Norway, Hungary and France in the early 11th century is the best example of this.

Early-medieval Russia appears to have been inspired mainly by Byzantium. But at that time, Byzantium was also a shining example for many Western European countries and was the most prestigious successor of the Roman Empire. Christianity came to Kiev from Constantinople and not from Rome, but the eastern and western traditions within Christianity were still very closely linked at that time. Thanks to the Byzantine Christian culture, the Old Russia was initiated to the Ancient Greek, Ancient Roman and Ancient Hebrew legacies that formed the foundations of what is called *European civilisation*. The images of King David, Hercules and Alexander the Great in the stone reliefs of the Cathedral of St Demetrius in Vladimir (1194-1197), as well as the Roman-esque elements in 12th century Russian architecture bear witness to a high level of like-mindedness between the different European cultures of the day, from France and Italy to the north-east of the Russian state. Today's historians ascribe an increasing importance to the cultural stimuli that Old Russia received from Central Europe, the Balkans and Scandinavia. Of course, one must not underestimate the influence of Persian, Turkish and, later, Mongolian elements, but there is in no way an equilibrium. The Christian tradition that unites Russia with its neighbours in Europe has always played a decisive role in Russian cultural history.

The Mongolian invasion signified a certain amount of discontinuity. The further disintegration of Russia and the long-term Mongolian oppression between the 13th and the 15th century weakened the cultural contacts with Central and Western Europe and caused a considerable increase in Eastern influences. Nevertheless, this general picture must be refined. Even in this period of Mongolian rule, the principalities and city-states in the western part of Russia, above all the two main trade centres Novgorod and Pskov, continued their cultural exchange with their neighbours in Europe. In those centres, Mongolian influence is far less noticeable than the influence of the North German Hanseatic cities. The city of Novgorod, which at that time controlled large areas in the North of Russia, remained wide-open to the West during the Mongolian period. And elsewhere in Russia too, where the Orthodox Christian culture continued unabated, the general European spiritual tradition was never lost.

After 1480, with the reintegration of the Russian country under the leadership of Moscow, not only the Mongolian rule came to an end, but also the independent role of Novgorod as the mighty trade partner of Lübeck, Hamburg, Stockholm or Bruges. This age-long port to the West was closed almost completely, but at the same time other, new openings emerged. The Muscovite state under Grand Prince Ivan III made noticeable contacts with the Greek and Italian culture. The Italian architects who around 1500 expanded the Muscovite Kremlin, the centre of power of the Third Rome, symbolically reconfirmed Russia's European orientation. Together with England and France, 16th century Russia was on its way to absolute monarchy. No matter how many eastern, Asian elements influenced the Muscovite court and in the day-to-day life of the Russians, politically, economically and culturally the country looked much more to the West. Tsar Ivan the Terrible competed with the German emperor; he sought contacts in England and wanted to recapture Russian access to the Baltic Sea to have closer ties and more relationships with Western Europe; he gave important privileges to English and Dutch merchants who had found their way to Archangel.

In the 17th century, even before Peter the Great, Russia's diplomatic and trading relationships with all of Europe down to Spain were so extensive that the cultural and psychological contact grew considerably. The inspirational power of the European cultures (e.g. Poland, Germany) was noticeable in education as well as in military skills, in architecture and even in the art of icon painting. The ties with Turkey, Persia or Central Asia were also important to the Russians, but were never echoed in their culture as much as the European connections. At the level of ideas, there was of course a high level of mistrust of the Latin, catholic, western world. Objectively speaking, however, the modernisation of Russia inspired by Europe was already in full swing by the 17th century, albeit in the beginning in a spontaneous and chaotic manner.

Around 1700, Peter the Great consciously tried to fundamentally integrate his country into Europe. He did not want to make Russia a part of Western Europe, he wanted to make his country as modern, strong and powerful as the rest of Western Europe at that time, for which it had to borrow many elements from Western civilisation. Although the empire of the Tsars expanded to the Pacific Ocean, Siberia was colonised and treaties were concluded with China, Russia did not try to find its place in Asia, but instead among the European superpowers. The descendants of Peter the Great increasingly involved their empire in the *Concert of Europe*. Without reservations, the Russian political elite joined the large European family of rulers, aristocracy and the highest official-dom. But conflicts appeared as well. Both during the War of 1812 with Napoleon and during the Crimean War with Great Britain and France (1853-1856) people in Russia had the impression they were fighting against Europe. These wars did not last long, however, and after both wars tsarist Russia was closely involved in all European political activities again. It regarded itself as the eastern vanguard of European civilisation which the Russians – as they and some Western Europeans thought at the time – started to spread in the Caucasus, Central Asia and the Far East, like the English in India and the French in North Africa.

Particularly Russian culture lived with its face towards Western Europe. Most styles, forms and ideas came from the West, including the idea that Russia *does not* belong in Europe. From the end of the 18th century, a new cultural and psychological type of person was formed in the intellectual elite: the Russian European, a free, rational and open-minded person who felt spiritually related with his fellow Europeans. Many famous names in Russian culture can be listed here as striking examples of this Russian European: Karamzin, Pushkin, Turgenev, Chaikovsky, Rakhmaninov, Vladimir Solovyov, Berdyaev and others. Apparently, this process of Europeanisation went off faster and was more intense in the aristocracy and in the circles of the intelligentsia than in the large sections of the Russian population, which stuck to traditional ways of life. Until well into the 20th century, the traditional way of living and the folk culture of the Russian people had little to do with modern Western European civilisation. It can be compared, however, to the early, not secularised, archaic folk culture of rural Europe. In that sense, the Orthodox-Christian peasantry of Imperial Russia is in its own way European too.

During the golden half century after the abolition of serfdom, between 1861 and 1917, when Russia's economic and cultural development was remarkably fast, the opening to other European countries was bigger than ever before. Russia outside Europe? A dualistic country with *European* and *Asian* elements? The official Russia placed itself (for the last time in 1914) consciously and without the slightest uncertainty in the company of the great European superpowers and looked down disapprovingly on Asia and even on Japan. The Russians saw Asia from the point of view of a European colonial power. Social groups in Russia, no matter how diverse politically, from dignitaries to revolu-tionaries, searched for ideological and cultural stimuli in Western Europe. The Russian conservatives emulated the reactionary policy of Austria-Hungary, the liberals had always been anglophiles, while the revolutionaries liked to take their example from their French and German comrades.

After many other inspiring western ideas, Marxism was finally adopted. However, with the Bolshevik October Revolution of 1917, Soviet Russia became more isolated from the rest of Europe than the medieval Russian principalities had been under the Mongolian yoke. Nevertheless, European orientation was not entirely lost. The prevailing Marxist ideology was inspired by Europe and used – albeit only in theory – many western concepts and values: freedom, democracy, self-development of every human being, as well as rational and scientific thinking. The Soviet Union dwelled on 'proletarians of all countries' and hoped for the revolutionary awakening of Asia and Africa, but the Marxist books always referred to the old Europe, the cradle of the revolutions: the barricades of 1848, the labour movement in England and Germany, the Parisian Commune, the socialist parties throughout Europe. Even unintentionally, the communist ideology reminds the Russians of a common European tradition, of the European sources of inspiration. In a way, no matter how paradoxical it may sound, the role of Marxism in the Soviet Union can be compared to that of the Christian heritage in medieval Russia: a spiritual link with Europe.

In addition to this spiritual link, there was a more practical, economic link. The communist leaders wanted to modernise their country and during that process of modernisation in the twenties and the thirties, they did not look at Asia, but at Western Europe and North America. Lenin and Stalin made no secret of their wish to impart the Russian worker with a bit of solid German pragmatics, combined with a bold American approach and initiative. No matter how repellent the Soviet ideologists found the West, they kept referring to examples of capitalist Europe, not only to scientific and technical innovations, but also to certain European values as willingness to work, efficiency, rational organisation, thrift, etc. After Stalin's death in 1953, Soviet citizens were permitted sparse travelling abroad, during which they had to study all the useful elements of European civilisation in order to introduce those elements into the new communist society. Not one word on Asian values or Asian experiences. In the Soviet Union, people talked a great deal about the solidarity with poor, courageous Asian nations in their fight against American imperialism. However, nobody ever thought of learning something from them.

Finally, the opposition to the communist dictatorship also sought inspiration and moral support in Western Europe and America. From the sixties onwards, the concept Europe is the symbol of freedom and of all the political and social ideals of the dissidents and of the steadily growing numbers of critical young people. To most of them, liberalising and even radically changing the communist system meant in fact returning to Europe. The Russian cultural elite in the Soviet Union after Stalin's death eagerly tried to closely follow the developments in different European cultures: Polish and Italian cinema, French literature, or British pop music. Modern Western European literature was hardly ever published in the Soviet Union; instead, many famous classics were translated. In reading and rereading Dickens and Balzac, the average Soviet citizen strolled through the legendary streets of London and Paris, listened to famous dialogues and established a sentimental relation with a Europe that he had never seen, but that aroused great fascination.

In the sixties and seventies, again thanks to stimuli from the European neighbouring countries, the Russian intelligentsia also discovered Indian philosophy, Chinese poetry and Japanese art. Yet, for most Russians, the interest in Asian cultures remained a superficial and elitist fashion, while the cultural orientation towards Western Europe and America was more or less widespread, sentimental and all-embracing (literature, cinema, art, fashion, tourism, languages, political and social events and ideas, values, manners and habits). Just like in the 19th century, the Russian intellectual from the Soviet period lived with his spirit in Europe, preferably in France or England. And it was as a self-conscious European that he sometimes showed an interest in the exotic, Asian East.

4. Mentality

How European is the mentality of Russians today? Many authors still see substantial cultural and psychological differences between the people on the western and eastern sides of Europe. What are the most notable differences revealed in the day-to-day lives of the people?

It is well known that Russians in general are less individualistic; they are less cut off from one another. They easily appeal to each other in all kinds of situations. Privacy or any other boundaries between equals are respected less in Russia. For a Russian, his fellow man is not really a sovereign microcosm; a Russian feels that he has a natural right to the attention and solidarity of others. For instance, people openly and voluntarily discuss each other's personal financial problems and freely borrow money from their friends. Because of the many collectivist reflexes, Russians grant each other less individual freedom to act and have more difficulty outlining and following their own individual way in life.

The totalitarian communist dictatorship denied its subjects every form of social and economic independence for 70 years. The sense of initiative and the spirit of enterprise did not get a chance to develop. The social apathy and passiveness are a heavy burden for today's Russia. Instead of trying to change

126

their lives and take care of themselves, too many people just keep waiting for a solution from above or for help from someone else.

There are also important differences in the work culture and time planning. Russians do not feel comfortable with a regular, strictly measured work rhythm. They would rather not work like machines, but instead with ups and downs, alternating between long breaks and outbursts of activity. Clearly, the prestige of working is lower than in most western countries. That working hard usually results in a successful career is far from obvious to Russians. As far as time planning is concerned, arranging, planning and preparing everything ahead of time is not popular in the former country of the five-year plan culture. Writing down appointments in a diary was highly unusual in Russia until recently. Psychologically, the Russians also leave a great deal of room for the unplanned, the unexpected, and they do not believe that you can keep everything under control all the time. The proverbial Russian fatalism is far from extinct. It is indeed a wise philosophy, but too often it paves the way to social lethargy.

Furthermore, with regard to social roles of men and women, Russian society is much more patriarchal than western society. A macho spirit runs rampant in Russia in every domain. The paternalistic attitude towards women is not strange to young people, either. Although, in major cities at least, tolerance for all kinds of minorities has increased over the past few years, racism, xenophobia, homophobia and sexism are still a matter of course in Russia. This is one of the reasons why Russian society is much more discordant and violent. A huge amount of social energy is lost every day to all sorts of conflicts between ordinary people. The western political correctness and the whole western culture of compromise and conflict management still have a very long way to go in Russia.

These and many other elements make Russian mentality differ so much from what is usually called European mentality. Of course, it is open to discussion whether one can define this so-called European mentality and whether one can apply that definition in the same way to the whole of Western and Central Europe. There may be so many gradations and varieties that the contrast with the Russian mentality is eventually less sharp and less visible. However, of more importance is the dynamic aspect: the evolution. The cultural and psychological differences in mentality between Russians and their fellow Europeans are very often comparable to the differences between modern capitalist and traditional pre-capitalist mentality. Many peculiarities in Russian mentality were quite common in other European countries in the past. But in Western Europe, and to a lesser degree in Central Europe as well, modern capitalism has caused enormous changes, especially in the 20th century. For Russia, all those developments and changes are still to come.

Are most differences just a matter of time? Someone who claims that the Russian mentality is not European might be better off saying not yet. The development of capitalism in Russia over the last ten years has caused fast and radical changes in the life style of tens of millions of people. A growing number of Russians, first and foremost the young ones in the large cities, begin to react and change their lives and begin to take care of themselves and plan their own individual lives and careers. Especially in their attitude towards planning a career, doing business, getting a degree, making money, planning a future, having a relation, etc, these young people – even after such a very short period of time – are less different from their peer group in Western Europe than they are from their peer group in Soviet times. Mentality adapts amazingly fast to changing life styles. The ease and casualness with which this adaptation takes place may of course differ from region to region, but it is very clear which direction Russia is heading. Differences in Russian and European mentality are gradually fading.

5. Language and Spontaneous Sentiments

Europeanisation is accelerated considerably by the conscious or subconscious adoption of western customs, fashions and expressions. Never before has the Russian language been so open to borrowing foreign, mainly English, words. The openness of the language shows an openness of spirit; it stands for an open mind. But is this Europeanisation or Americanisation? Because of the fact that we have to deal with fundamental elements of western civilisation, this last issue is not relevant yet. However, let us not forget that geographically Western Europe is much closer to Russia than the United States of America and therefore more important for business relations, tourism and all kinds of exchanges. The traditional cultural orientation of Russia, which has always been focused on its European partners, is another argument for using the term Europeanisation. If a Russian of the modern growing middle class has his apartment or office renovated – according to the latest western trends, of course, and using imported materials only – this will be called *yevroremónt* in Russian, literally 'renovation in a European way'. And if a Russian refers to something very modern and of the very best quality, he will call that *yevrostandárt*, 'European standard'; again, and for good reason, referring to Europe.

This brings us to our final theme: Russian sentiments with regard to Europe. Both inside and outside Russia, there are various ideas and myths that situate the country a bit further away from Europe and somewhere halfway between Europe and Asia. People talk about *Eurasia*, which, God knows why, according to the same theory is immanently in conflict with everything that is European. There is some speculation about the meaning of Russia's age-old coat of arms: does the two-headed eagle not look equally towards Asia and Europe?

(If this interpretation is right, then it applies first of all to the empire of the Habsburg dynasty, because the Habsburg imperial two-headed eagle is much older; in all probability, the Grand Prince of the Russia from the 15th century did not take his symbol from the Byzantines, but from the German emperor). Moreover, there is a fashionable geopolitical theory that declares Russia, as a perfect example of a continental power, to be a natural opponent to the *Atlantic*, seafaring Western Europe. Russian politicians and journalists like to lecture on a multi-polar world, in which Russia has to look politically and ideologically towards Asia in order to constitute, together with China and India, an anti-pole to the US and the EU.

But when we switch from the ideological and political level, to the level of language and spontaneous sentiments, we find something that is inconsistent with all those theories and political constructions. A Russia that balances between Europe and Asia and looks in both directions symmetrically? The Russian language knows better.

The concepts *European* and *Europe* are highly prestigious in Russia. They are associated with the highest level of development, with the civilised way of life or of doing things, with the best quality and with respectability. Something like *It is a European work* is an emphatic and enthusiastic expression of praise that outstrips all others. *Europe!* exclaims the Russian, somewhat ironically or not, when something happens in a nice and correct way or when he steps into an elegant or just a very tidy room. *He is educated in a European way* does not mean that the person had his education and training abroad, but that he or she is well-educated and well-trained, erudite and a connoisseur of languages. *You are really European*: there is no bigger a compliment you can make a Russian. And all these expressions belong to an old tradition: already 200 years ago the word *yevropéyets, European,* was used for a highly civilised person, for a *bearer of the highest form of civilisation,* a *Kulturträger.*

The concepts *Asian* and *Asia* are antonymous to this, strongly negative and disapproving. Asian means barbaric, uncivilised, coarse, underdeveloped and even wild. A hotel in Russia may be called *Yevropeyskaya* or *Yevropa,* never *Asiatskaya* or *Asiya.* Already in the 19th century, the concept *Asian* in all discussions implied underdevelopment, backwardness and even barbarism; *European,* on the contrary, stood for civilisation and progress. *Asia!* is what the Russian says disdainfully when he encounters unorganised, wild situations, uncultivated people or just dirty streets and places. *Asian* can be a term of abuse in Russian, a serious insult. Just try and call a Russian an Asian, even if he lives in the Far East, i.e. in Asia. He will react with incomprehension and anger, as if he was slapped in the face. He may live only a few kilometres from the Chinese border, yet he would not even think for a single second that he is in Asia.

This unique sensitivity that is expressed in the use of words says a great deal about the cultural and psychological orientation of the Russians. The use of language shows a spontaneous, perhaps subconscious choice for Europe, not for some theoretical dualistic and actually anti-European construction like *Eurasia*.

Because Russians traditionally paid more attention to what was European than to what was Asian, and because they valued what was European much higher, they see European traditions and European reality as something which they are already familiar with and which is already partly theirs. In the eyes of a Russian, everything that is European is prestigious, fascinating, from time to time moving. In Russian papers, *Age-old gothic stones* or *The tiles of Old Europe, wetted by rain* are standard phrases, which are striking because of their tenderness.

There is another sentiment that plays a major role here. The Russians feel that they have protected and rescued Europe several times during the course of history. They acted as a protective shield against the Mongolians in the 13th century, saving European civilisation from terrible destruction. And did they not free Europe from Napoleon and from Hitler? Some people in Russia take their list of real or alleged benefactions a step further and even consider Moscow's current battle against Islamic extremism in the Caucasus and Central Asia to be a modern form of Russia's traditional defence of Europe. While reality may be far more complex, it is the simple feelings of the people that determine the unique sentimental relationship Russians have with the Europe they have always defended and liberated.

The fact that Russians have focused on Europe for ages now does not mean, however, that they do this without any psychological difficulties or complexes. Russians have mixed feelings towards the Western and Central European countries. Compared with Russia, these countries are so small and so densely populated that on the one hand, Russians look at them with a feeling of superiority and pity them to a certain degree. Sometimes they just laugh about the puppet theatre in those tiny little countries with their minor little problems. Russians are quite sure that only Russia has real and serious problems and they are convinced that only the Russian people have enough strength and enough stamina to overcome the real difficulties. On the other hand, they look at their Western neighbours with a strong feeling of inferiority, because most European countries are rich, modern and well-organised welfare states. Sometimes this leads to blunt and rude reactions and provocative behaviour and sometimes to silly humbleness towards fellow Europeans. Russians, finally, may feel undervalued in Europe, among other things in their historic role as saviours of European civilisation, and they talk about the ungrateful Europe. In other words, these are complicated, subtle feelings that are typical of people who want to belong to something, but feel that they do not quite fit in yet and are therefore not totally accepted.

Nevertheless, the Russians have always had close contacts with Asian countries, too. Many Russians actually lived in the former Soviet republics in Central Asia or fought in Afghanistan. In recent years travelling to Turkey, the United Arab Emirates and even China has become routine for Russian business-men. Asian traditions and the Asian reality, however, are still a bit strange and incomprehensible for Russians. Russian people have little interest in Asia. With regard to their Asian neighbours, Russians do not have any intricate complexes, just a high level of indifference, a sense of superiority and alienation. Worse still, the Asian *East* is something the Russians have never felt comfortable about, culturally nor psychologically. The expression 'you never know with the East' from a popular Soviet film is one of the most frequently quoted expressions in the contemporary Russian press. For the average Russian, everything Asian is not only alienating, but also even alarming and frightening.

What Russians share with all Europeans are certain Eurocentric sentiments: the inherent frustration of *the scared white man* and the great fear of Asia and everything outside the familiar world of white people. It is of course a less pleasant theme than European ideas and inspirations in Russian culture, but it is reality. From an objective point of view, Russia has been attacked more from the west than it has from the east. Nevertheless, the historical fear of the Mongolians, Turks and Chinese lies much deeper in the Russian heart. The expression 'the yellow peril' can be found throughout Europe, but the Russians have a whole range of extremely negative clichés about Asia, which – ironically – coincide exactly with what many a westerner thinks about Russia: a far away world, strange and dangerous, primitive, backward, dirty, violent, barbaric, fanatical. This is partly why the Soviet Russians in the seventies were much more afraid of China, to which they were ideologically related, than they were of all the NATO countries combined. A war with China not only seemed more dangerous, but also much more realistic, because it would be a war between two completely different civilisations that rejected one another. All the cultural and psychological premises for such a war already existed. Ordinary Soviet citizens had the feeling that a Chinese invasion would mean a real war of destruction, a complete catastrophe. A favourite theme in Russian black humour of the time was that, rather than the Americans having their hamburgers, the Chinese who would someday be eating their dinner with chopsticks in Moscow's Red Square.

Paradoxically enough, many Russians have even stronger Eurocentric sentiments and phobias than the average European. After all, Russia was isolated from the outside world for a long time and the Russians are still not used to strangers the way Western Europeans are. The Russians have, for obvious reasons, far less experience in travelling around the world, they are far less familiar with foreign cultures and they do not have any experience with conscious multiculturalism. The Russian racism towards Asians and Africans is usually not a conviction, but a naive and primitive reaction from a nation that has been isolated and psychologically removed from the rest of humanity for far too long. To put it mildly, this spontaneous, emotional Eurocentrism of the Russians, their distrust and fear of the Asian East do not form a firm basis for all the theories and political strategies which place Russia outside Europe and push it into the arms of authoritarian Asian regimes in order to isolate it from general European development.

In the last decade, various opinion polls have tried to determine which nations the Russians have the most sympathy for. The first seven places are taken by European nations (Belorussians, Ukrainians, Bulgarians, French, Fins, Serbs and Italians). The Japanese are the first Asian nation and they are the only Asian nation among the first twelve. But in the eyes of the Russians they form an exception, being more Western than real Asians. These polls, once again, confirm that Russia is emotionally drawn to Europe. As stated earlier, the relationship is full of complexes and hurt feelings. Very often Russians will get angry with their European neighbours and grumble: *We will show Europe*. They never want to show Asia anything. Psychologically, they are constantly involved with Europe. No partnership with China and India and no political flirt with Iran or Iraq can weaken Russia's centuries-old and sentimental relationship with Europe. Thanks to its historic development and the logic of its modernisation, its cultural traditions and its spontaneous sentiments, Russia – from the Baltic Sea to the Pacific Ocean – is inextricably bound together with Europe.

THE ROLE OF THE ORTHODOX CHURCH IN THE FORMATION OF THE RUSSIAN SELF-CONSCIOUSNESS

Ioann Ekonomtsev

The second millennium has come to a close, as are the great celebrations of the 2000th anniversary of the advent of the Lord our Saviour Jesus Christ. The birth of Christ became the starting point of our calendar and laid the basis for the extremely rich Christian culture, which formed the national self-consciousness of the peoples of Europe. In 2000 the Russian Orthodox Church celebrated this anniversary together with all the Russians. Many national and international high officials from both Church and state organisations attended these celebrations. In the forums not only reverend bishops took part, but also secular scholars from around the world, senior representatives of state institutions, ministers and high representatives from the armed forces. The culmination of the jubilee celebrations of the Russian Orthodox Church was the Synod of Bishops and the festive consecration of the Cathedral of Christ our Saviour[1], rebuilt thanks to the efforts of the entire population.

1. Orthodox Belief and Russian National Identity

The scale on which the 2000th anniversary of the birth of Christ our Saviour has been commemorated clearly shows that Orthodoxy continues to occupy a remarkable place in Russian society. Why this is so, can easily be explained. Nations form over many centuries and are influenced by various factors, situations and conditions. The self-consciousness of a people is in fact the spiritual luggage that has been gathered during its entire existence and is the experience and the sufferings the people lived through and compiled over these centuries. The history of Russia is indivisibly intertwined with that of the Russian Orthodox Church. If we study the formation of the self-consciousness of our country, we notice that it is the Orthodox Church that acted as a symbol for the country's national uniqueness over a period of one thousand years. The history of Russia shows that throughout the centuries there has been a close tie between the Orthodox belief and national identity in the minds of the Russian people.

The powerful state of Kievan Rus was a direct result of the Russian conversion to Christianity. The Slav pagan cults, which existed in Russia until its conversion, mainly regulated the relationship between man and nature. They could not serve, however, as a basis for the formation of a society and a state. In the 9th and 10th century Russia was traditionally tied to Constantinople.

These ties played an important part in the choice of Prince Vladimir. More than 1000 years ago, the capital of the Russian territories, Kiev, was christened, and other cities in Kievan Rus followed: Chernigov, Novgorod, Rostov, Polotsk … Orthodoxy gradually became the leading religion in the territories of the Russian state of that time. Russia also adopted the supreme Byzantine culture. The Russian people did not only become part of the family of European peoples, they also acquired the high ideals of the Christian State and the Christian moral code. Historians report that the first schools in our country studied mainly the Holy Scripture and the works of the church fathers. The first books to be translated into our language were the Gospel, the Scriptures of the prophets and the apostles. The first works written in Russia are hagiographies, works on the lives of the saints. Virtually the entire early Russian literature is permeated with Orthodox themes. One cannot but be amazed by the maturity of the mind, the depth of the emotions, the abundance of theological information and the oratory achievement shown in the most important work of the 11th century by metropolitan Hilarion of Kiev titled *"Sermon on Law and Grace"*. Drawing the attention to the superiority of the Evangelic Law and of the Christian faith, the author discusses its distribution among all peoples and, particularly, among the peoples of the Russian territory. The book ends with an extensive prayer to God in which Hilarion calls on God in the name of the entire Russian territory: *"We are a flock that You started to watch over not long ago … continue to bestow Your kindness on Your people; strengthen the peace; reward famine with affluence. Ensure that our rulers frighten the world; make the boyars wise; spread our cities; nurture Your Church; look after Your property."*[2] These words, which express the thought that the Russian soil is God's property, were valued so much that they were still used in church services in the 16th century.

In the 13th century, the Russian territories were occupied by the Tatar-Mongols. Extreme poverty burdened the Russian territories for a few centuries. By that time, the Orthodox faith had become deeply rooted in the Russian national self-consciousness. The perception by the people of the burden of the Tatar-Mongolian yoke is ample evidence of this. The scriptures and the description of lives of that time show that no one doubted that the Tatar-Mongolian yoke was God's punishment for the sins of the people, and that therefore, penance and a change in lifestyle were required in order to defeat the enemy.

It was in the Orthodox Church that the Russian people found support in distress and sorrow. Moreover, it was precisely this Christian belief that gave the Russian people the feeling that they were different from the oppressor and that they were superior to them. In the time of the Tatar-Mongolian yoke, the Russian people were more than once in a position to testify to their devotion to the Christian faith and the Orthodox Church. In 1246 for example, Khan Batu summoned the Prince of Chernigov and demanded that he walk through fire and bow to the sun and several idols before entering the palace-tent of the Khan, as was the Mongolian custom. The noble Prince refused, saying that he as a Christian could not bow to idols. When he was given the choice either to bow or to die, the Prince did not hesitate to choose the latter. This is certainly not the only example that can be given. Many Russians shared his fate. In defending themselves against the attacking enemy, the Russian people were convinced that they shed their blood and died mainly for the Orthodox faith and for the Orthodox Church. While he was accompanying his troops out of Moscow to go and fight against the Tatar-Mongols, Dmitry Donskoy said: "We are going to fight the godless and profane Khan Mamay for the sake of the true Christian religion, the holy Church and all Christianity."[3]

2. Orthodox Belief and the Unification of the Russian State

The liberation from the Tatar-Mongolian oppression and the rise of Moscow, which had gathered Russian territories around it, is connected with the name of Saint Sergey of Radonezh. Among the heroes of the battle at the Kulikovo Field we can distinguish Aleksandr Peresvet and Rodion Oslyabya – monks and warriors, who fought with cassocks over their armour. And it was not just the Russian combative heroism that had religious features. The hard labour, the daily life and the Russian enlightenment also shared these specific religious features. One can hardly overestimate the role of the Russian Orthodox Church in uniting the territories around Moscow and forming a unified, single Russian state. The Church invariably sanctified the authority of the central government; the clergy acted as referees in arguments between the princes and between a prince and his city. The system of one church organisation for the entire state with a single centre which appointed bishops to the various cities, that had been adopted from the Byzantine empire, objectively served as an important political shadow structure. It helped the centripetal forces counter the centrifugal ones. The importance of the city in which the metropolitan resided grew.

The Christian ideals of holiness were deeply embedded in all layers of the Russian society. Historians report that it was customary in ancient Russia to take monastic vows before death. Most princes honoured this custom. The majority of them even subjected themselves to the strictest monastic rule. Examples include Aleksandr Nevsky, his wife and children, Ivan Kalita and Michail Tverskoy, as well as practically all the *posadniks* (governors of city-states), the rulers of Novgorod, the boyars from Moscow and many others.

The Church always took responsibility for the most varying aspects in the lives of the Russian people and it was customary for the Tsar and the boyars to attend Church Synods. While referring to the needs of the fatherland, the Tsar frequently addressed the church fathers with a speech, posing them a number of questions they were supposed to answer. The decisions of the Church Synod in the Moscow period regarded practically every aspect of both state and church government and judicial system. The Church Synod in 1551 for example, which received the name *Stoglavy* because the work it produced consisted of 100 chapters, discussed measures to end disorder and lawlessness not just in church matters, but also in worldly matters. The deeds of the Synods naturally extended into those of the state. For the new Code of Law Tsar Ioann IV (i.e. Ivan IV) requested the opinion and approval of the Stoglavy Synod. Ivan IV invited all the bishops with many of the clergy to participate in the meeting of the State Duma, which gathered in Moscow, in order to decide on whether or not to stop the war against Poland. In matters of the utmost importance, for instance when he had the intention to declare war on his enemies, the Tsar usually requested the blessing of the metropolitan, the bishops and the entire consecrated Synod. When Grand Prince Ioann III (i.e. Ivan III) headed his troops to go and fight the Tatar Khan Akhmat and hesitated whether or not to start the battle, the Synod of Russian Bishops sent the Grand Prince the message to courageously stand up for faith and fatherland.

With his spiritual authority the head of the church always tried to act for the benefit of the country. Sometimes he went to the Tsar and instructed him in both church and state obligations; he sent messages to appanage princes trying to convince them to bow to the Grand Prince and not to break the oath they had taken nor the agreements they had entered into and not to shed Christian blood in vain. He warned against treachery of the Court of God and threatened with excommunication from the church. As head of the church, the metropolitan of Moscow appeared before the worldly ruler in a capacity of mediator to express regret for those who had done something wrong or who had fallen into disgrace and asked forgiveness for them. When necessary the Church could also denounce the state rule. Metropolitan Filipp, for instance, severely criticised the Oprichnina.[4] His courageous condemnation of the practices of the Oprichnina resulted in his dying as a martyr.

Another traditional obligation of the head of the Russian Orthodox Church was to appeal to the warriors to fight courageously for Tsar and country. The Russian Church often blessed the soldiers before they were sent off to participate in a war to liberate the people. In 1380, for instance, Saint Sergey of Radonezh blessed the Russian troops headed by the holy Prince Dmitry Donskoy before they went to fight the Tatar-Mongolian oppressors. In 1612, bishop Gergomen, Patriarch of Moscow and all Russia, blessed the volunteer corps on their way to fight the Polish interventionists. At the time of the war against the French invaders in 1813, the Moscow bishop Filaret said in his congregation: "If you evade death for the honour of faith and fatherland, you will die a criminal or a slave; die for faith and fatherland and you will receive life and a halo in heaven".[5]

In the beginning of the 19th century, the victorious war against Napoleon was being waged. In the same period, the Russian classical literature appeared, which played an important role in the development of the national self-consciousness. Karamzin, the author of the famous *"History of the Russian State"ъ*, is rightly considered the creator of the modern Russian language. He truly felt the needs of the time and was able to express the Russian national consciousness in distinct forms and historical narratives. The moral pathos of the so-called 'Russian thinking' starts with Karamzin. For the historian Karamzin, history was the school for moral education of the people, because it handed down the testament of the forefathers onto the offspring and offered an explanation for the present and an example for the future.

3. Orthodox Belief and the Self-Consciousness of the Russian People

In the same period, the first attempts at philosophical reflection on the position of Russia and the Russian people in the family of the whole of mankind appear. The official formula of the Russian national self-consciousness was introduced by the Minister of Education under Tsar Nicholas I, Sergey Semenovich Uvarov. In 1832, he launched his well-known triad: *Orthodoxy, autocracy and narodnost,* in which narodnost stands for the national character, the national traits of the Russian people. According to Uvarov, this triad in itself contained the essence of the national self-consciousness. Other thinkers who dedicated parts of their works to the question of the people's self-consciousness are Aleksey Khomyakov, Ivan Kireevsky, Yury Samarin, metropolitan Filaret, Fyodor Dostoevsky, Konstantin Leontiev and many others. Although their approaches are quite different, one cannot but notice that the basic spiritual and religious element in their reflections on Russia and the Russian people is the most important, leading and determining one. Without the spiritual reading, without the Orthodox Church, the content of their reflections about the self-consciousness of the people becomes empty and pointless.

One of the problems Slavophiles are confronted with is the correlation between general values common to all mankind and national values. Today, we are still being confronted with this important problem. According to Aleksey Khomyakov, the truth common to all mankind can only be reached by adhering to the specific ideals of one's own people. In this way the above mentioned narodnost becomes, as it were, the guide to the truth common to all mankind. A human being stripped from all national ideals and specific characteristics cannot freely acquire values common to all mankind; his life is poor and fruitless and it is necessarily aimless and empty. Only through national values does the concrete expression of values common to all mankind become apparent. In Khomyakov's opinion narodnost is "the basis which is common to all mankind and which is enveloped in the everyday life of a people", and therefore "serving this narodnost is to a high extent serving the cause of all mankind". Khomyakov was convinced of the fact that Russia is strong due to the truth of its spiritual basis, because "the root and basis of the cause is religion, and only the clear, conscious and complete celebration of Orthodoxy will open up the possibility of any other development".[7]

The most important theme by far for Russian philosophers is the fate of their country and, of course, the way in which that country will develop. This theme is expressed in their reflections on the 'Russian Idea'. The very expression *Russian Idea* came from Fyodor Dostoevsky. Dostoevsky frequently turned to this theme throughout his creative works. Many philosophers wrote articles and books on this Russian Idea – Vladimir Solovyov, Nikolay Fyodorov, Vasiliy Rozanov, Nikolay Berdyaev, Sergey Bulgakov, Nikolay Lossky, and Ivan Ilyin.

Dostoevsky thought world-wide empathy to be one of the main characteristics of the Russian people, i.e. the ability of the Russian individual to respond to other people's burden, to feel this burden to be his or her own, the ability to help others and to enjoy the happiness of others. *"The Russian soul ... is the genius of the Russian people; of all people it might be the Russian people that is most suited to internalise the idea of the unity of all people, of brotherly love, the idea of a sober attitude, which is willing to forgive animosity, which can see and forgive the unreasonable, a view that will iron out inconsistencies and contradictions".*[8]

Vladimir Solovyov, who adopted these thoughts on the national vocation of his predecessors and developed them further, underlines that the Russian Idea "in itself is nothing exclusive, that it is merely a new aspect of the basic Christian idea".[9]

4. Forcefully Imposed Atheism Leads to Crisis

For Russia, the 20th century was a difficult time with many severe trials and disasters. The country underwent serious social changes; it suffered a civil war and a period of repression; it saw the disintegration of the single state and it recently underwent economic and political disorder again. For the Church, this 20th century was a period of the worst persecution ever, conducted by atheists to destroy the belief in Christ. Thousands of cathedrals and churches were destroyed, the educational system within the Church was wiped out, as well as the missionary and charity work. The mighty power of the state machinery was used to root out the Church from the people's lives, to raise a wall between the Orthodox faith and all spheres of social life: between faith and science, faith and culture, faith and education, between faith and bringing up young people in society, between faith and creating a fighting spirit in young soldiers.

In Soviet times, a marxist-leninist atheist ideology was forcefully imposed by the communists in the name of the people. In this totalitarian state, all efforts were directed at creating a new human being, at making the word *Russian* identical to the word *Soviet*. Unfortunately, they were to a certain degree successful in their efforts.

In spite of the fact that in the last years of Soviet rule the falsity of the communist ideology became clearer every day, and in spite of the fact that people had stopped believing in the marxist-leninist dogmas and communist ideals long before the collapse of the socialist system, a substantial part of the population had been violently cut off from the Church for too long. Under the heavy burden of the atheist regime, the Russian people had moved away from the Orthodox church and, as a result, very often lost its traditional moral values. The communist rule led to the weakening of the one national self-consciousness of the Russian people.

The lack of national self-consciousness in the Russian people today is without doubt one of the main reasons for the crisis in Russia. Unfortunately, a specific part of the population of Russia today is indifferent to the fate of the rest of the population and this part only passively takes part in the processes taking place in society. The loss of the idea of one single nation is one of the symptoms of our time, as is the disdain to national cultural traditions and the dissolution of the own culture into artificial pseudo-cultures, which is a process in which the people at the same time lose their roots. All scholars agree that the national identity of the Russian people today is quite vague.

For every sensible human being it is obvious that without overcoming the moral disintegration it is impossible to restore the country. Gradually, we are beginning to realise that the spiritual vacuum and the absence of clearly determined moral values is leading the country straight to downfall and destruction. Every society needs a spiritual basis in order to become and remain closely knit. What can we resort to in difficult times of trial and crisis? What is holding our society together? What can put a stop to the growing number of social conflicts and new tensions?

A well-developed self-consciousness is one of the instruments with which the country can get out of this crisis and can be reborn. National ideals determine the direction the country is going in and give substance to the people's lives. When these ideals are not present or alive among the people, this very people will sooner or later destroy the very roots of its existence, and as a result put an end to its historical existence. The national self-consciousness of any people includes respect for its own history, knowledge of its own culture and the continuation of the best traditions and customs. The presence of a certain notion, idea, a concept of oneself, of one's own place in the world's development are integral parts of a developed feeling of identity.

5. Orthodox Belief Leads out of Crisis

After the Soviet Union had fallen apart and the Soviet ideology had died, people in our country felt the need to think about what was the source of the meaning of their lives, to think about what kind of answer could be given to questions like: What are we living for? What is the meaning of life? And it is not surprising that in the process of shaping a national identity the people first of all thought of Orthodoxy. Despite the fact that the Russian Orthodox Church proclaims its principle of non-interference in political matters and has no intentions whatsoever of playing a role in political or state matters, Orthodoxy invariably instils trust in people and has an unconditional authority among the citizens in society. The Church is an important stabilising factor in social life and in uniting the Russian people around common moral priorities like justice, patriotism, peacemaking, creative work and family values. After the collapse of the Soviet Union, the Church remains one of the last spiritual bases that helps people unite in the post-Soviet period.

Again this is not surprising – throughout the entire tragic 20th century the Orthodox Church was one with its people, in happy as well as in sad times. In the awful period of repression, in Stalin's camps and prisons, hundreds of thousands of clergymen, monks and laymen paid tribute to God in dying as martyrs and in accepting their hardship and sufferings in a submissive way. Last year, many of them were canonised by the Synod of Bishops. The heroic deeds of these martyrs and confessors became the solid basis of the resurrection of the Orthodox Church that we see today. The flame of repression was not only unable to destroy the Christian faith, it even strengthened the Church and it tempered the hearts of its true children. In the years of repression and persecution, Orthodoxy appeared to be the moral support for the majority of the Russians. And without exaggerating one can say that it is the spiritual values of Orthodoxy and the Orthodox upbringing over the centuries that helped the people of Russia in a very substantial way to endure the wars and the sufferings in this 20th century. These values made the impressive achievements of the Soviet Union possible, achievements in economy, in politics, in social life, in science, achievements in war, and in many other areas. The foundations for the real achievements of the socialist state – such as free education, free medical care, the successes in space and in science in general – had already been laid to a large extent in pre-revolutionary times; they were based on pre-revolutionary Russian traditions.

Man always turns back to his national sacred things, and in Russia that is Orthodoxy. People cannot break the ties with what was sacred on the soil where they were born and where they grew up. *"We consider ourselves to be members of a nation"*, says Sergey Bulgakov, *"because we really belong to that nation, we are part of it as of a living organism. And this very belonging of ours is in no way dependent on our consciousness; it was there before there was a consciousness, it exists alongside this consciousness and it even exists in spite of it. This belonging is not merely the beginning of our consciousness or our will, quite on the contrary, it is rather this consciousness of nationality and this will to have it that forms the basis for the belonging to come into existence"*.[10]

In recent years, a lot of sociological research in our country has been aimed at finding out what the relation our population was towards religion. The result of this research struck the scientists because of one regularity. 94% of Russia's population stated that their relation to Orthodoxy was *good* and *very good*. Moreover, 82% of all Russians stated that they were followers of the Orthodox faith. According to the same research, however, only 50% of the population of this country consider themselves to be believers. But even those who do not believe in God and who do not belong to the Church, somehow consider themselves related to Orthodoxy and give credence to those values and moral imperatives that are traditionally defended by the Church.

6. Social Concept

The Russian national self-consciousness is evident in the spirituality of the people, in its religious values, its system of moral criteria, its strong moral principles and in its civil responsibility. And it is exactly these values and principles that the Russian Orthodox Church calls upon today. The fact that the Synod of Bishops accepted the document called *"Bases of the Social Concept of the Russian Orthodox Church"*[11] may be seen as one of the most important events in church and social life in Russia. This document presents the attitude of the Orthodox Church towards several developments and processes in modern society. More specifically, the Social Concept explicitly says that the Church calls upon its flock, upon its true children, to take active part in social life, and that this active life must be based on the principles of the Christian morals. Orthodoxy is first and foremost the way to save the soul, but because the Church has a higher goal for mankind, it gives sense and meaning to all aspects of earthly life. Trying to live according to spiritual values does not mean that matters of state and society are of less importance to the Christian. For Christians, a manichaean aversion to live in the world around him is intolerable. The Christian takes part in life because he understands that the world, the society, the state are all objects of the love of God himself, for they are all meant for transfiguration and purification on the basis of a God-commanding love. The inseparable church organism takes part in that worldly life to its full extent. The Church accomplishes the mission of saving mankind through good works (charity, philanthropy), aimed at improving the spiritual, the moral and also the material situation in the world. In not directly trying to convert all people to the Orthodox belief, the Church is convinced that common charity brings the people who give and the people who take to the knowledge of Truth, that common charity will help them preserve or restore the correct God-given moral standards and norms and that it will bring them closer to peace, understanding and prosperity, under which conditions the Church can do its Saviour's work in the best way.

The Social Concept also brings up the question of the mutual relations between Church and nation. The Church in its very nature has a universal, and hence, a supranational character. The Church does not divide people on the basis of national characteristics nor on the basis of class: in the church – this is what the Apostle Paul writes in the third chapter of his epistle to the Colossians – there is neither Greek nor Jew, circumcision nor uncircumcision, Barbarian, Scythian, bond nor free: but Christ is all, and in all".[12] The universal character of the Church does not mean, however, that Christians do not have a right to national originality, to national self-expression. On the contrary, the Church unites the universal beginnings with the national ones.

The Social Concept ranks patriotism very highly. The Orthodox Christian is summoned to love his homeland and his blood brothers. Such love is one of the means to fulfil one of God's Ten Commandments – the Commandment that "thou shallt love thy neighbour", which includes the love of one's own family, fellow tribesmen and fellow citizens. The patriotism of an Orthodox Christian must be effective. It manifests itself in protecting the fatherland from the enemy, in working for the sake of one's country, in organising a social life, which includes taking part in governing the country. The Christian is simply summoned to preserve and develop his national culture and the self-consciousness of his people.

In our modern multi-confessional, multi-national and multi-ethnic society, the Russian Orthodox Church plays its most important role in the field of peacemaking. National feelings may lead to and have in fact not seldom given rise to sinful occurrences, such as aggressive nationalism, xenophobia, exclusion on the basis of nationality and interethnic conflicts. In the end, these phenomena very often lead to the deprivation of the human rights of individuals as well as of the rights of a people as a whole, and to war or other acts of violence. Orthodoxy never has been and never can be considered the national religion of the Russian people. The Social Concept clearly states that it is strongly contradictory to Orthodox ethics to divide people into good and bad, or to belittle certain ethnic minority groups. Doctrines that put a nation in the place of God or reduce the religious belief to one of the many aspects of national self-consciousness are totally incompatible with Orthodoxy. In the fight against such sinful phenomena, the Russian Orthodox Church is realising an extremely important mission: the mission of reconciling nations that have been drawn into hostile conflicts.

7. Orthodoxy is the Core of Russian Culture

Today's spiritual impoverishment, this spiritual gap, cannot be filled by merely borrowing from Western culture; western values can never fill that gap. And it is not without reason that Aleksandr Isaevich Solzhenitsyn insists on telling us that Western liberal values cannot catch on in Russia, cannot find acceptance in Russia, for they do not fit the deep needs of the Russian people. The situation in Russia is a special one. The spiritual ideals of the people have been moulded by the Russian Orthodox Church for ten centuries. Russian culture and Orthodoxy are in their essence indissoluble. The Orthodox religion is the core of Russian culture. The Church is the sole social institution that remained unchanged for centuries. Orthodoxy brought us the written language, literacy and statehood. And that is why Orthodoxy – as a universal Russian religion, as a typical and traditional Russian religion and as a religion that forms culture – simply has to manifest itself today as a creative and uniting spiritual power. One can say that the Russian Orthodox Church represents the national traditions and the historical legacy of Russia, and it is for that reason that the Church has the duty to take on the mission of the forming of a national self-consciousness and identity.

Notes

1 In 1812 Tsar Aleksandr I ordered the construction of the cathedral of Christ our Saviour to mark Russia's victory over Napoleon. It was considered to be one of the most powerful symbols of Russia's spiritual identity and nationhood. The cathedral was destroyed by Stalin in 1931. In 1994, mayor of Moscow Yuri Luzhkov ordered the reconstruction of the cathedral of Christ our Saviour. The ceremony of consecration of the completed Cathedral was held on September 1997 during the celebration of the 850th anniversary of Moscow.

2 Mitropolit Kievskiy Ilarion, *Slovo o zakone I blagodati*. Bogoslovskie trudy, sb. 28, Izdanie Moskovskoy patriarkhii, 1987, str. 340.

3 Mitropolit Makariy (Bulgakov), *Istoria Russkoy Tserkvi*. T.3, Otdel 1, Gl. VII, Sostoyanie very i nravstvennosti, Izd-vo Spaso-Preobrazhenskogo Valaamskogo monastyrya, Moskva, 1995, str. 309.

144

4   Private court or household created by Tsar Ivan IV the Terrible (1565) that administered those Russian lands (also known as *oprichnina*) that had been separated from the rest of Muscovy and placed under the Tsar's direct control. The term also refers to the economic and administrative policy that divided the Russian lands into two parts: the *oprichnina* and the *zemshchina*.

5   Khristianskoe verouchenie o voyne i voinskoy sluzhbe. In: *Zhurnal Moskovskogo Patriarkhii*, 1999 g. Nr. 8.

6   Karamzin N.M. *Istoriya Gosudarstva Rossiyskogo*. Sankt Peterburg, 1842-1844, 4 vol.

7   Khomyakov A.S. *Polnoe Sobranie Sochinenii*, t.3, Moskva, 1900, str. 228-229.

8   Dostoyevsky F.M. Pushkinskaya Rech. *Polnoe Sobr. Soch.*, t. 26, Leningrad, Izd-vo Nauka, str. 129-130.

9   Solovyov V. *Russkaya Ideya*. Per.s fr. G.A. Rachinskogo, Bryussel, Izd-vo Zhizn s Bogom, 1964, str. 32.

10   Bulgakov S.N. *Iz razmyshleniy o natsionalnosti*. Moskva, 1914, str. 3.

11   For the full text in English translation, see: http://www.russian-orthodox-church.org.ru/sd00e.htm

12   The Holy Bible, New Testament, Colossians 3.11 – King James Version 1611, American Bible Society.

DOING BUSINESS WITH THE RUSSIAN FEDERATION: LEGAL AND REGULATORY ASPECTS OF EXPORTING TO RUSSIA

Koen Vanheusden

Business strategies should be based on a proper market analysis and should reflect the reality that the company will be facing, not just a personal perception of this reality. As such, any business strategy towards the Russian Federation requires a thorough understanding of the socio-economic reality underlying this political entity. And there is more to reality than what meets the eye.

What is surprising when one examines the attitude of Belgian businessmen towards the Russian Federation, is that their strategies are often more based on their perception of reality, of the stories they hear, than on reality, i.e. on the facts and figures themselves. For many Belgian companies, the 'Wild East' starts at the Russian-Polish border (until the mid-nineties it started at the German-Polish border); civilisation ends where the CIS starts, where the Mafia reigns, where there is no law and order, where the law of the jungle holds sway.

Although the facts and figures as they will be presented do not draw an overall positive impression of the Russian economic reality, we should not forget that for European businessmen, Russia is the only market left to conquer that can be reached by truck. Now that positions have been taken in Central Europe (the candidate member states), for European enterprises there is no other market of significance left where they have a permanent competitive advantage over their traditional competitors (USA, Japan and even China). Distance and its consequences regarding logistics, transport costs, transport risks, and time are the only production factors that cannot be downsized by a more efficient business organisation and new machinery. Distance and its consequences are the only advantageous production factors that cannot be copied by competitors. Thus the Russian Federation is of importance to European industries, and will continue to be of importance.

1. Exporting to the Russian Federation: Facts, Figures and Future[1]

Often statistics only examine the values of the goods exported and imported. However interesting this may be for macro-economic purposes, a comparison between the values and the volumes of goods traded in gives far more insight into the relationship between trading partners.

1.1. European Union Exports to the Russian Federation

In terms of the value of the trade flows, the Russian Federation is the European Union's 26th largest customer. If trade between the member states of the EU is not taken into account, it is Europe's 12th largest customer. It is Europe's 4th largest customer in Central and Eastern Europe (after Poland, Czech Republic, and Hungary).

EU exports to the Russian Federation(in 1000 EUR)²						
Order of importance	1992	1993	1995	1997	1999	09/2000
1.	841247501	84 2785310 24.2%	84 3288787 20.4%	84 4572517 17.9%	84 3088494 21.4%	84 2916168 22.3%
2.	8643942.5	87 704867 6.1%	85 1411493 8.7%	85 2479919 9.7%	85 1210425 8.4%	85 1238186 9.5%
3.	85 295526 5.2%	85 689652 6%	87 813671 5%	87 1466467 5.7%	02 946980 6.5%	87 789182 6%
4.	8828365.8	10 552649 4.8%	90 762749 4.7%	94 989416 3.9%	87 742951 5.1%	39 559965 4.3%
5.	8727128.3	22 517583 4.5%	94 731846 4.5%	02 851787 3.3%	39 538420 3.7%	48 472480 3.6%
6.	1024793.9	90 429661 3.7%	22 603203 3.7%	39 848596 3.3%	94 512404 3.5%	94 443990 3.4%
7.	7223453.8	64 349405 3%	18 460537 2.9%	90 778020 3%	90 486506 3.4%	90 415769 3.2%
Total % of total	571522853	11528121 52.3	16133497 49.9	25539262 43.5	14460018 52	13054633 52.4
Evolution		1.026	+39.9%	+ 58.3%	-43.4%	

LEGEND:

1st line: product
02: meat and edible meat
08: edible fruit and nuts
15: animal or vegetable fats
16: preparations of meat
17: sugars and sugar confectionery
22: beverages, spirits (vodka ...)
30: pharmaceutical products
38: miscellaneous chemical products

39: plastics and plastic products
57: carpets
72: iron and steel
84: machinery, boilers and electromechanical equipment
85: electrical machinery, apparatus, ...
87: cars, trucks ...
2nd line: .000 KG
3rd line: % of total

The relative stability that the Russian Federation represents for the top three exported products is surprising. For some other products (mostly food products) the Russian Federation seems to be a much less stable market. Also remarkable is the strengthening of the position of machinery as Europe's first export product. This could be an indication that the Russian Federation is importing more and more capital goods, which would suggest that the economy is recovering.

The following table presents the statistics on the volumes that the Russian Federation is importing from the European Union: meat is Europe's first export product (9.2%), followed by cereals (8.6%), products of the milling industry (7.3%) and salt and sulphur (5.1%).

These figures prove the importance of the Russian Federation for Europe's ailing agricultural sector. They also prove that the macro-economic conclusions based on value statistics are not always confirmed by the day-to-day realities. The trade in food products creates many more problems in the realm of logistics, traffic organisation, border crossing, certification and employment than would be expected on the basis of the value statistics.

Comparing values and volumes, Europe was exporting an average value per ton of 2241 EUR for the first 9 months of 2000. In 1999 Europe exported to the Russian Federation an average of 1815 EUR/metric ton. This evolution confirms the increasing weight of investment goods (that have a higher value per volume than food products) in Europe's export package.

EU exports to the Russian Federation (in 1000 KG)		
Order of importance	1999	09/2000
1	Cereals (10) 1426423	Meat and edible meat (02) 534799
2.	Meat and edible meat (02) 1149446 14.5%	Cereals (10) 501399 8.6%
3.	Animal or vegetable fats (05) 533359 6.7%	Products of the milling industry (11) 426271 7.3%
4.	Products of the milling industry (11) 440010 5.5%	Salt and sulfur (25) 299607 5.1%
5.	Articles of iron and steel (73) 374339 4.7%	Paper and paperboard (48) 284049 4.9%
6.	Paper and paperboard (48) 316659 4%	Edible fruit and nuts (08) 254604 4.4%
7.	Inorganic chemicals (28) 253309 3.2%	Ores, slag and ash (26) 253630 4.4%
Total	7938697	5824776
% of total	56.6 %	43.9%
EUR/1000 kg	1815	2241

1st line: product
2nd line: .000 EUR
3rd line: % of total

1.2. Belgian Exports to the Russian Federation

From a value perspective, the Russian Federation is Belgium's 25th largest customer. If trade with the other member states of the EU is not taken into account, it is Belgium's 11th largest customer. It is Belgium's 3rd largest customer in Central an Eastern Europe (after Poland and Hungary).

The level of Belgian exports to the Russian Federation is much more volatile than Europe's: from 1992 to 1995, vodka was Belgium's first/second export item, but since 1997, it has disappeared from the top 7. The same happened with carpets, which were Belgium's number one export product from 1993 to 1997, and then the market collapsed. After a steady rise beginning in 1993, meat preparations were Belgium's number two export in 1997, and then they disappeared from the charts.

This volatility explains to a large extent the reluctance of Belgian businessmen to invest in the Russian Federation. Their 'investments' tend to be limited to franchise agreements, licenses etc., i.e. strategies that do not involve substantial financial engagements but only non-monetary (intellectual property) inputs.

A second important remark is that the Russian Federation has until recently – and contrary to the overall EU statistics – primarily been a market for Belgian consumption goods, and not for investment goods, although in its overall statistics Belgium has a very significant level of production and export of capital goods (machinery, transport equipment). Surprisingly, the structure of the Belgian export statistics does not reflect the European statistics, and Belgian trade with Russia is quite different from Belgium's trade with its other trading partners.

Because of this export structure (consumption goods instead of capital goods), Belgian exports have been much more sensitive to economic developments and their incidence on purchasing power in the Russian Federation. Moreover, because of the nature of the goods exported, Belgian exporters seem to be less familiar with long-term financing necessities (consumption goods are often paid in advance and require different financing delays than capital goods), they deal not only with established clients but also often with small Russian companies, and they are often confronted with less transparent situations (under-invoicing).

The growing importance of capital goods (that allow the creation of local added value, production and employment) in Belgium's export package towards the Russian Federation confirms the recent turnaround in the Russian economy. This is reminiscent of some of the countries of Central Europe (Poland, Hungary) that, shortly after the fall of the planned economies, spent the savings from the past to import consumption goods, combining this with a steep economic decline (1991-1995). Only when capital goods gained importance in the import statistics (from 1996-1997 onward) was the economic decline stopped. (Think of the Polish example, with several years of strong economic growth on its track record).

BE-exports to the Russian Federation (in 1000 EUR)						
Order of importance	1992	1993	1995	1997	1999[3]	2000
1.	22 23641 13.5%	57 101428 20.5%	57 196434 24.4%	57 187341 13.4%	15 91145 13.4%	84 161524 17.2%
2.	84 23330 13.4%	22 72328 14.6%	22 87726 10.9%	16 122509 8.8%	10 64520 9.5%	39 91147 9.7%
3.	17 17830 10.2%	17 38753 7.8%	15 53661 6.7%	39 93829 6.7%	84 61127 9%	30 83247 8.86%
4.	87 15898 9.1%	84 28746 5.8%	85 44878 5.6%	15 92310 6.6%	38 60332 8.8%	15 66303 7.1%
5.	72 13936 8%	87 26803 5.4%	16 35367 4.4%	87 81876 5.9%	39 58149 8.5%	08 63729 6.8%
6.	15 7579 4.3%	85 24787 5%	84 30978 3.9%	30 72958 5.2%	30 35697 5.2%	85 46542 4.9%
7.	57 7538 4.3%	16 17147 3.5%	87 26314 3.3%	84 72737 5.2%	08 29929 4.4%	57 45140 4.8%
Total	174392	493778	804180	1397859	682732	939798
% of total	62.8	62.6	62.5	51.8	58.8	57.4%
Evolution		+183%	+62.8%	+73.8%	-38.7%	+47.83%
% of EU-exports to RU	3%	4.3%	5%	5.5%	4.7%	4.7%

LEGEND:

1st line: product

02 : meat and edible meat
08 : edible fruit and nuts
15 : animal or vegetable fats
16 : preparations of meat
17 : sugars and sugar confectionery
22 : beverages, spirits (vodka ...)
30 : pharmaceutical products
38 : miscellaneous chemical products
39 : plastics and plastic products
57 : carpets
72 : iron and steel
84 : machinery, boilers and electromechanical equipment
85 : electrical machinery, apparatus, ...
87 : cars, trucks ...

2nd line: .000 KG

3rd line: % of total

In volume, animal and vegetable fats were Belgium's first export product (18.6%), followed by edible fruit and nuts (17.2%), plastics (9.6%) and meat (8%).

BE exports to the Russian Federation (in 1000		
Order of importance	1999	2000
1.	Cereals (10) 450580 49.9%	animal or vegetable fats (05) 104284 18.6%
2.	Animal or vegetable fats (5) 144786 16%	Edible fruit and nuts (08) 96174 17.2%
3.	Edible fruit and nuts (08) 48998 5.4%	Plastics and plastic products (39) 53705 9.6%
4.	Meat and edible meat (02) 46409 5.1%	Meat and edible meat (02) 44844 8%
5.	Plastics and plastic products (39) 40563 4.5%	Products of the milling industry (11) 44444 7.9%
6.	Carpets (57) 14200 1.6%	Sugars and sugar confectionery (17) 33102 5.9%
7.	Preparations of meat (16) 9300 1%	Carpets (57) 20866 3.7%
Total	902069	559291
% of total	83.7 %	71%
Evolution	+ 42.6 %	- 38%
EUR/1000 kg	1640 (1998) 704 (1999)	1680 (2000)

1st line: product
2nd line: .000 EUR
3rd line: % of total

In 1998, Belgium exported an average of 1640 EUR/metric ton. This average dropped significantly after the August 17, 1998 crisis to an average of 704 EUR/metric ton in 1999. (Once again, Belgian trade reacted much more intensely to the economic situation in the Russian Federation than EU trade). In 2000 the average rose back to 1680 EUR/ metric ton.

2. Russian Exports to the European Union

The Russian Federation is the EU's 14th largest supplier. Russia is Europe's 5th largest non-EU-supplier and the 1st in Central and Eastern Europe.

Russia's first export product, in value, is mineral fuels (59.5%), followed by iron and steel (5.8%), aluminium (5.3%), and diamonds (4.8%). Russia's first seven export items (out of a total of 99) account for nearly 85% of the country's income from trade with the EU.

RU exports to EU (in 1000 EUR)		
Order of importance	1999	09/2000
1.	Mineral fuels (27) 11747992 53.4%	Mineral fuels (27) 16168834 59.5%
2.	Aluminum (76) 1236226 5.6%	Iron and Steel (72) 1579629 5.8%
3.	Diamonds(71) 1198044 5.4%	Aluminum (76) 1445377 5.3%
4.	Iron and Steel (72) 1161423 5.2%	Diamonds(71) 1314727 4.8%
5.	Wood and articles of wood (44) 1090841 4.5%	Wood and articles of wood (44) 992569 3.7%
6.	Inorganic chemicals (28) 819388 3.7%	Nickel (75) 971234 3.6%
7.	Nickel (75) 628582 2.9%	Inorganic chemicals (28) 554758 2%
Total % of total	21983285 81.3 %	27154591 84.8%
Surplus	7,525,986	14,099,958

1st line: product
2nd line: .000 EUR
3rd line: % of total

Contrary to the EU export statistics, where value and volume statistics are different, the statistics on Russia's exports, based on the volumes traded in, confirm the value statistics: mineral fuels (75.8%) are Russia's first export product, followed by wood (10.1%), iron and steel (5.5%), and salt and sulphur (1.6%). The first seven export items represent 96% of Russia's total exports to the EU.

RU-exports to the EU (in 1000 KG)		
Order of importance	1999	09/2000
1.	Mineral fuels (27) 107146172 76.7%	Mineral fuels (27) 84937942 75.8%
2.	Wood and articles of wood (44) 14343694 10.3%	Wood and articles of wood(44) 11368637 10.1%
3.	Iron and Steel (72) 7082262 5.1%	Iron and Steel (72) 6176422 5.5%
4.	Salt and sulfur (25) 2252638 1.6%	Salt and sulfur (25) 1747406 1.6%
5.	Fertilisers (31) 1913032 1.4%	Fertilisers (31) 1712136 1.5%
6.	Ores. slag and ash (26) 1370104 1%	Ores. slag and ash (26) 939519 0.8%
7.	Aluminum (76) 1023339 0.7%	Aluminum (76) 888848 0.8%
Total	139731556	112072547
% of total	96.7%	96%
EUR/1000 kg	157	242

1st line: product
2nd line: .000KG
3rd line: % of total

In 1999 Russia exported an average of 157 EUR/metric ton to the EU. This is only 8.6% of the average EU-exports. In September 2000, due to the rise in oil prices, this average had risen to 242 EUR/metric ton, which equals 10.8% of the average EU-exports.

3. Russian Exports to Belgium

The Russian Federation is Belgium's 17th largest supplier. It is Belgium's 9th largest non-EU-supplier and the 1st in Central and Eastern Europe.

Russia's first export product to Belgium, in value, is mineral fuels (30.6%), followed by diamonds (20%), then organic chemicals (8.6%), and then iron and steel (8.5%). Russia's first seven export items (out of a total of 99) account for almost 58% of the country's total income from trade with Belgium.

RU-exports to Belgium (in 1000 EUR)			
Order of importance	1998	1999	2000
1.	Diamonds(71) 303396 31.1%	Diamonds(71) 284452 27.8%	Mineral fuels (27) 466938 30.6%
2.	Mineral fuels (27) 238178 24.4%	Mineral fuels (27) 270636 26.5%	Diamonds (71) 305941 20%
3.	Iron and Steel (72) 63730 6.5%	Iron and Steel (72) 69339 6.8%	Organic chemicals (29) 131510 8.6%
4.	Inorganic chemicals (28) 44744 4.6%	Organic chemicals (29) 55059 5.4%	Iron and Steel (72) 129123 8.5%
5.	Fertilisers (31) 43913 4.5%	Wood and articles of wood (44) 51261 5%	Aluminum (76) 67131 4.4%
6.	Salt and Sulphur (25) 37779 3.9%	Aluminum (76) 45707 4.5%	Nickel (75) 60531 4%
7.	Aluminum (76) 36459 3.7%	Fertilisers (31) 38660 3.8%	Wood and articles of wood (44) 59669 3.9%
Total	974935	1022029	1526299
% of total	78.8%	58.8	57.4%
Evolution		+4.83%	+49.34%

1st line: product
2nd line: .000 EUR
3rd line: % of total

The statistics on Russia's exports to Belgium, based on the *volumes* traded in, indicate that mineral fuels (55%) are Russia's first export product to Belgium, followed by salt and sulphur (10.3%), iron and steel (9%) and fertilisers (7%). The first seven export items represent 95% of Russia's total exports to Belgium.

RU exports to Belgium (in 1000 KG)		
Order of importance	1999	2000
1.	Mineral fuels (27)	Mineral fuels (27)
2.	Salt and sulfur (25) 618094 12.6%	Salt and sulfur (25) 543791 10.3%
3.	Wood and articles of (44) 349203 7.1%	Iron and Steel (72) 478048 9%
4.	Iron and Steel (72) 333186 6.8%	Fertilisers (31) 373739 7%
5.	Fertilisers (31) 317322 6.5%	Inorganic chemicals (28) 284480 5.4%
6.	Inorganic chemicals (28) 149562 3%	Wood and articles of wood (44) 268757 5.1%
7.	Organic chemicals (29) 129007 2.6%	Organic chemicals (29) 189238 3.6%
Total	4905867	5278492
% of total	95.8%	95.5%
Evolution	+ 1.3 %	+ 7.6%
EUR/1000 kg	208	289

1st **line:** product
2nd **line:** .000KG
3rd **line:** % of total

On average, Russia exported 201 EUR/metric ton to Belgium in 1998. This was only 12.3% of the Belgian exports average. In 1999, this average remained stable (208 EUR/metric ton) but it rose substantially compared to the Belgian value/volume average (29.5%). This was probably a consequence of the financial crisis in August 1998 which, combined with the dioxine crisis, weighed heavily on Belgian exports to Russia.

Thanks to the rise in the oil prices, Russia's average rose to 289 EUR/metric ton in 2000, but it declined as a percentage of the Belgian value/ton (1.2%). Over the years, the average value per volume of Russia's exports towards Belgium has constantly been higher than the averages for its exports to the EU. The diamond trade can easily explain this. As this item is much more important in Russia's trade with Belgium than in its trade with overall Europe, it influences the average substantially.

4. Comments

Statistical information always has to be handled with great care. This is even more the case with statistics on trade with the Russian Federation. A survey performed by the Belgian Foreign Trade Board in 1998 indeed showed that the Russian statistics on their imports from Belgium gave a total import value of only 59% of the corresponding Belgian export statistics. For Russia's trade with Switzerland, the statistics differed by 15% in the same direction. These differences can be explained by under-invoicing, but are still too important to simply be ignored.

Looking at the statistics only, the structure of the trade relations between the EU and Belgium, on the one hand, and the Russian Federation on the other hand, have the characteristics of trade relations with a developing country. Russia is an exporter of low value raw materials and an importer of high value food, consumption goods and finished products; all the added value is produced in the EU.

Trade with Russia is highly volatile, its export products are very sensitive to 'world prices' and the country has to export enormous volumes of non-renewable natural resources to finance its imports.

This perception explains why Belgian businessmen consider granting credit to Russian commercial partners a risky business and require advance payments when exporting to Russia. It also explains why they are sensitive to requests for under-invoicing, why Belgian business strategies towards the Russian Federation are often more inspired by opportunism than by strategy, and why Belgians are trying to limit their financial exposure in Russia and are therefore not ready to invest either in the Russian Federation or in supplementary production capacities for this market.

The perception of Russia as a developing country, which is based on the foreign trade statistics, is confirmed by the internal socio-economic problems the country is facing:

- Russia has known no economic growth since 1989 (GDP 1999 = 1989 x 57%).
- Poverty in Russia is growing; (19% of the Russian population earns less than 2.15 USD/day).
- Customs officials earn on average 20 USD/month.
- Russia is one of the few countries in the world where life expectancy is declining from year to year (58 years for men, as compared to 74 years in Belgium).
- The workforce is often paid in kind.
- The average age of capital goods is 20 years.
- Communication with the administration inevitably means red tape.
- The Russian privatisation process is often defined as the 'capitalisation of future corruption' instead of as a means to render more efficient state services.
- Russia's tax collection system is completely insufficient. In spite of draconian tax legislation, the Russian state gets only 15% of its income from tax collections. In the EU this percentage is 60%, and in the USA even 85%. In Russia, customs duties account for 40% of state revenue.
- Russia often has problems meeting its foreign debt payments, though the amount of Russian capital on foreign bank accounts exceeds Russia's foreign debt.
- FDI in Russia is very low, as few risk their money in the Russian Federation.
- Russia is generally considered to have insufficient regulation, and to be plagued with corruption and poor rule of law.

In the eyes of many Western businessmen, doing business in Russia has become synonymous with dishonesty, bribery and tax fraud. The motto is: "take the money and run". This state of affairs has turned the optimism of perestroika into a policy of "Forget Russia".

These perceptions have vast consequences for the way Belgian businessmen approach the Russian market. Because they believe there is no rule of law in the Russian Federation and they distrust the Russian administration and judicial system, they do not 'organise' their Russian business activities – they 'arrange' them.

Because they are convinced everything can be 'arranged', they lack respect for the Russian administrative formalities. Because they think under-invoicing is normal, they become vulnerable to corruption. Because they consider Russia to be the 'Wild East', they limit their engagements, they require prepayment when exporting, they require payment after delivery when importing, and they disregard administrative obligations.

Nevertheless, as much as Europeans blame Russia's problems on the Russians, the Russians themselves often hold the West responsible. Russia's socio-economic disintegration started in 1992 when it embraced the market economy. Capitalism introduced corruption, the profits of corruption are held in Western bank accounts, and Western businessmen pay out the corruption money. The West uses the Russian Federation as a market for exporting low quality products, for polluting production, etc.

A New Wind?

The year 2000 marked a change, for which the new President is regarded to be the catalyst: the Russian economy recovered much more strongly than expected after the rouble crisis in late 1998. Real GDP growth rose 7.7% and industrial production 9% in 2000, owing to three factors in particular:

1. The sharp (78%) decline in the value of the rouble against the USD between August 17, 1998 and January 13, 2000 cut imports sharply and encouraged import substitution. Since then the exchange rate of the RUR has stabilised.

2. The sharp rise in the price of oil – and the inability to afford imported goods as a result of the precipitous decline in the RUR's value – helped the value of Russian exports to expand rapidly and provided a substantial trade surplus of close to USD 60 billion in 2000, up substantially from USD 36.2 billion in 1999. This in turn has eased concerns about Russia's ability to service its foreign debt (in February 2000 the Duma allowed payment of all debt at that time owed to the Paris Club) and has resulted in substantial positive ripple effects into the domestic economy.

3. A tight monetary policy in the wake of the rouble devaluation prevented hyperinflation and permitted a significant reduction of interest rates. As a result, Russian enterprises have been freed from some of the severe liquidity constraints experienced earlier. Thus, there has been a significant move away from barter and towards settlement in cash and a reduction in the level of payments arrears.

For the first time in a while, Russia seems to have a more competent government. It needs to use the current opportunities to relaunch economic reforms in order to make the recovery more sustained. The rush of good economic news coming from Russia indeed conceals the poor performance of business investment, even though the foreign trade statistics indicate that fixed investment is beginning to pick up. Without a strong revival of business investment and Russian manufacturing competitiveness, it is improbable that the

Russian economy can continue sustained growth over the medium term at the levels needed to raise living standards and employment.

And the Future?

Nevertheless, Russian policymakers face urgent problems. One of them is the country's dependence on world energy prices. The strength of the recovery owes much to the spectacular rise in oil prices. If these cool down, so will the Russian economy.

Another matter of concern is inflation. During the past two years, the authorities have succeeded in bringing down inflation from 86% at the end of 1998 to probably less than 20% by the end of this year. Nevertheless, the recent increase of the inflation rate will have to be tackled; or else the situation will worsen.

Presently, 2003 is being pointed to as the next most likely financial crisis,[3]

- firstly, as foreign debt will accelerate from 6 billion USD in 2001 to 18 billion USD in 2003,
- secondly, as non-monetary settlements still account for 1/3 of all transactions between domestic industries and in-kind swaps account for over 1/5 of all domestic sales
- thirdly, because the overall infrastructure (telecommunication, outdated equipment, collapsing power lines, unreliable electricity supplies) has become obsolete and will put pressure on domestic production. As almost half of the energy bills going to industry are not being paid, the question is where the money will come from to finance the necessary investments in the power sector
- Ultimately, if the rise in domestic consumption that is fuelling the current growth of domestic production comes to an end, the question will arise as to what will solve the approaching economic problems. It is uncertain whether increased oil and natural gas exports will be sufficient.

Notes

1   Based on the Intrastat statistics (97 chapters of the Harmonised System), information on trade between the EC and the Russian Federation available for the first nine months of 2000; information on trade between Belgium and the Russian Federation for the entire year 2000.
2   Source: Eurostat, following the 97 chapters of the custom's tariff.
3   From then on without Luxemburg.
4   Moors K.F. 'Concern Over the Reasons for Russian Economic Growth', *Russia/Central Europe Executive Guide*, 28/02/2001, Vol. 11, no. 4

Russia and the European Union: Towards a Strategic Partnership?

Katlijn Malfliet

Can we start this concluding article with a fairy tale? Little Red Riding Hood (the European Union) walked through the (post-Cold War) wood, with her basket full of the sweet things of post-war democracy and market building, bringing it to her European grandmother, Central Europe, situated in the old heart of Europe. This scenario, however, did not take into account the wolf. Unbeknownst to the unsuspecting Little Red Riding Hood, the big bad wolf had a plan to threaten the innocence of the little girl with his cunning tricks.

Is Russia that wolf with its big (nuclear) teeth? In an attempt to implement the so-called multipolar world concept, Russia has selected its strategic partners, and one of them appears to be the European Union. How then, exactly, can we understand this strategic partnership between the European Union and Russia? Or is the big wolf none other than the United States, trying to weaken the European Union as a growing economic competitor through NATO enlargement? Indeed it was a most strange experience that the first steps towards the dream of a united Europe were taken by NATO in its first enlargement wave. It cannot be denied that the NATO membership of three Central European countries opened the door for EU membership. Ten Central and East European countries have since then been selected as accession countries. However, the Summit of Nice clearly showed that the European Union is not yet ready for enlargement.[1]

Therefore, it is not unrealistic to start this introduction on a pessimistic note: not much is left of the post-Cold War dream of a "united Europe" and Gorbachev's idea of a "common European home". Was it perhaps wrong to build a larger Europe on Western European institutions and to largely leave to NATO its role as a transatlantic defence organisation? In relation to Russia, NATO enlargement policy is a major problem for building a united Europe. At the same time, however, no one can deny the need for NATO assistance in a developing EU security policy.

In the United States, the "Who lost Russia?" debate was one of the few foreign policy topics mentioned in the 2000 presidential race. The Republicans in Congress blamed the Clinton administration for just about everything that occurred in Russia. In the last days of Clinton's administration, insiders hit back in defence of the "Clinton legacy" in foreign policy.[2] In a different manner, the European Union, in its foreign policy towards Russia, is confronted with a confusing problem: Russia is for the European Union both a 'third' country and a legitimate player in the European territory. The European Union, as a geopolitical target region for Russia, has become the focal point of Russian policy. One could ask from a European Union perspective, "Why did we deserve Russia's love (and interference)?".

After all, the European Union and Russia (at that time embedded in the Soviet structure) denied each other's existence for decades.[3] We had to wait until 1988 before the Council of Mutual Economic Assistance (CMEA) and the European Communities recognised each other as legitimate institutions. Afterwards, however, mutual relations evolved rather fast. After the collapse of the Soviet Union a Partnership and Co-operation Agreement was concluded in 1994 between the EU and Russia. Relations with NATO developed in the framework of the Partnership for Peace and the NATO-Russia Council. However, the Kosovo crisis proved that NATO-Russia relations belong to a different discourse than EU-Russia relations. It is equally clear that the future security of the European continent will depend on the relations of the European Union with Russia.

In other words, Europe has a different stake in its relations with Russia than the US does. If not for NATO, the parties could almost certainly turn into each other's opposite, or at least one can say that their views are quite alienated from each other. One of the key shifts in Russian foreign policy under president Putin has been to take the European Union more seriously as an international player, moving from bilateral relations with Berlin, Paris, and London towards a dialogue with the European Union in Brussels as a political power in its own right. This policy shift is being driven by geography, economy and trade as well as by broader geostrategic calculations and the dawning realisation that the US under Bush is bent on downgrading relations with Russia. In this contribution, we limit ourselves to asking some elementary questions about the so-called "strategic partnership" between the European Union and Russia.

1. Who Took the First Step?

At the Köln summit in June 1999, the European Council launched its first Common Strategy towards Russia.[4] The common strategy was presented as a new policy instrument of the European Union towards third countries. The 1997 Amsterdam Treaty (which came into force in May 1999) did indeed broaden the foreign and defence policy instruments of the Common Foreign and Security Policy of the European Union. Although a common strategy needs to be accepted unanimously by the member states, its implementation (for example common actions) can be effectuated through majority decisions. In this way the European Union is endeavouring to harmonise the national foreign policies of its member states within an EU framework and achieve for itself a better balance in its policy towards third countries (non-EU members). Russia has been accorded the honour of being the first target country of this new strategic instrument. The Common Strategy presented to Russia a perspective of intensified co-operation and even of "strategic partnership". The term "partnership" referred mainly to the Partnership and Co-operation Treaty concluded in 1994: from the EU side it was the intention to refine the political dimension of this treaty, both conceptually and in its content. The term "strategic" referred mainly to the important security aspects of EU-Russia relations. EU insiders were less than enthusiastic, stating off the record that the 'common strategy' was contained nothing new in comparison with the Partnership and Co-operation Treaty, but that it was rather just a way for the European Council to work with a majority rule.[5] Afterwards, Javier Solana openly expressed what everyone was thinking: the Common Strategy was ineffective, too slow and lacking in innovative elements.[6]

Russia, in turn, responded to the EU Common Strategy with a "Medium-Term Strategy (2000-2010) for Development of Relations between the Russian Federation and the European Union".[7] In its response, Russia took the opportunity to formulate a well defined, conscientious and ambitious national foreign policy. Contrary to the EU Common Strategy, the Russian Medium-Term Strategy definitely brought a new approach to geopolitical strategy. The first level of discourse in the Russian Medium-Term Strategy communicated the message that Russia and the EU are economically interdependent and should therefore work together. At the same time, however, (in a second level of the discourse), Russia declared – for the first time and in a coolheaded way – that the European Union should respect Russian geopolitical ambitions, which are defined by Russia in a unilateral and non-negotiable way. This includes that the European Union should keep away from doing anything that is against Russian interests within the territory of the Commonwealth of Independent States and that the European Union should help Russia to regain influence in the Commonwealth of Independent States. In this way, EU partnership with Russia is becoming instrumental to Russian geopolitical aims. Afterwards, Russia further built on this basic approach by telling the European Union that it is not against EU enlargement, as opposed to NATO enlargement, but that its legitimate interests should be recognised in Central and South-eastern Europe, its former satellite countries. Kaliningrad, the future Russian enclave in an enlarged European Union, became the test case by means of which Russia was clearly showing that it has a stake in EU enlargement. It should be noted that the closing of borders will isolate Russia and that the European Union is defining its own aims in a rather contradictory manner: on the one hand it is proclaiming openness and a willingness to open up to new democracies, while on the other hand it is closing its borders in a frustrating way for the excluded countries.

Coming back to the question of "Who took the first step?", we must take into account the fact that, although the European Union formally took the first step, it was Russia that set the paradigms of a post-Cold War EU-Russia strategic partnership. The European Union approached Russia as a third country, not as a partner. It was Russia that defined the European Union as a "strategic partner", subordinated to Russian geopolitical aims. The notion of strategic partnership was clearly launched by Russia, which selected the European Union as one of its partners in an attempt to implement the so-called multipolar world concept. It is a clear sign that Russia under Vladimir Putin is beginning to strengthen its influence in the shaping of a new configuration of the international political space after the Cold War.

2. Who Is Who in the Strategic Partnership?

As in the fairy tale of Little Red Riding Hood, the personalities in this evolving geopolitical game are mysterious and, in a certain sense, disguised. A partner, as a matter of fact is someone you know very well, although he or she is different. The question, however, of who are the real partners in Euro-Russian relations is one of the most difficult to answer. Both partners are in continuous transformation. Both partners – the European Union and Russia – are in search of their own identity, and both are able to present themselves in several political disguises.

EC-CMEA relations (that was the way it all started in 1988) became EU-Russia relations after the collapse of the Soviet Union, instead of EU-CIS relations. This is quite a relevant fact in our discussions: Russia, in its identity perception and in its foreign policy ambitions, is clearly not confining itself to the borders of the Russian Federation; Russia is concerned with more than just CIS affairs. In its Medium-Term Strategy, Russia pointed out that as a geopolitical player it is looking differently at the question of state borders. Consulting the website of the Russian Council for Foreign and Defence Policy, one realises that the similarity to the European Union Foreign and Defence Policy is not confined to the name: Russia is behaving as a geopolitical power with its own ambitions and with a foreign policy relating to an identity that involves more than just a state.[8]

In this sense, the Russia-European Union project is closely related to the Russia globalisation project. But the same is true, in a reverse way, for the European Union. Behind the screen of a united policy towards Russia (the Common Strategy towards Russia), the European nations are pursuing their own agendas, (and within the different nations, each level of government is developing its own policy in what is referred to as "multilevel governance").

In that same line of thought, we may not remain blind to the fact that all former republics of the Soviet Union have become independent and sovereign states that make their own foreign policy choices. Their newly declared sovereignty can induce an important paradigm for renewed co-operation between the former Soviet republics. Their capacity for creating a Eurasian economic space based on new market principles is underestimated. This space could become a rather large market, with 300 million consumers, allowing each member country to work for it. Moreover, they could jointly uphold their interests in competition with other economic groups. It is not clear at this stage how further CIS integration will proceed: will it develop from a multi-state intergovernmental CIS basis, from a concept of progressing economic co-operation in the framework of a Customs Union, from regional co-operation such as GUUAM or the Central Asian co-operation, or through accession to the Russia-Belarus confederal structure? One thing is sure: Russia does not plan to be left without its own regional zone of influence.[9]

3. Shared Expectations

A partnership is based on trust. Trust in turn is based on shared values and expectations. Expectations should be answered in a proper way, otherwise the partner gets disappointed and co-operation becomes more difficult, if not impossible in the future. A partner needs respect. Respect for the fact that religion and democracy have an uneasy relation with each other, because religion has become (and always has been) an important identity marker for Russian statehood. Respect also for the fact that Russia is not a developing country. Because of lack of inspiration, EU assistance to Russia has been organised mainly in the spirit of the Lomé principles. Consultants who have worked in Africa or in the Third World were sent to Russia or the former Soviet republics "on the absolutely wrong principle that this is just applying the western model, be it in Africa, in Latin-America or in Russia".[10]

Russia is declaring that it is disappointed in the way Western help was provided to Russia. But the European Union in turn is reproaching Russia for not keeping its promises. In its Medium-Term Strategy, Russia is reacting reluctantly to the EU focus on democratisation, pluralism, rule of law, and common values. Domestic policy makes it difficult for Russia to accept this approach, even if it looks at the pragmatic side of partnership. Strategic partnership ends there, where the content and implementation of democratic values comes to the fore.[11] One of the best examples is the search for a political solution to the Chechnya crisis. At the core of the problem lies a different understanding of what "democracy", "human rights", "sovereignty", and "territorial integrity" really mean, both in a state framework and in international relations.[12] Russia reproaches the West that it does not understand what is happening in Chechnya: for Russia, Chechnya is about fighting terrorists, about integrity of state territory and about defending Christianity against Muslim fundamentalism. In this sense, Russia indignantly notes that the West should be grateful for Russia's efforts in Chechnya to defend the West against Asian fundamentalist tendencies (just as it stopped the Mongol invasion centuries ago). Another example was the Vienna OSCE summit, which ended without a final conclusion because, contrary to the engagement made by Russia at the OSCE summit in Istanbul one year earlier, it appeared to be impossible to fix a date for sending an OSCE observation mission to Chechnya.[13] Igor Ivanov, Russian minister of Foreign Affairs, answered by saying that the OSCE had transformed itself into a group of teachers, prescribing attitudes. One has to admit that in a real partnership one cannot accept that type of relation so typical for Euro-Russian relations: a relation between teacher and pupil.

4. Reciprocity

A partnership implies reciprocity. The concept of strategic partnership refers to a pragmatic-realistic co-operation between the European Union and Russia. European leaders are conducting themselves as if they held all the cards. This attitude, however, is not realistic. Russia has requested the European Union to be a provider of extensive funds for Russia and the CIS, though without offering much compensation in terms of political influence or priority for western contracts. On the other hand, the Europeans have become increasingly dependent on Russia for their supply of natural gas and they have become aware of the fact that Russia's economy is increasingly integrated with their own. Forty percent of Russia's exports are already going to the European Union. The process of EU enlargement will bring in 10 new member states from Central and Eastern Europe, and this enlarged grouping will absorb more than 70% of Russian exports.

Currently it is impossible to trace exactly what is going on economically in Russia and the CIS. Privatisation has created a "baroque" property structure, with commercial firms coming and going, changing the fate of former state property and setting out new links of interdependency. With a spate of mergers and acquisitions rapidly reshaping the face of Russian industry, some economists fear that giant corporate conglomerates with powerful political ties similar to the South Korean industrial groups called "chaebols" could come to dominate the country. A Boston-based professor in International Relations put it like this: "Right now, Russia is buying oil concessions in Iraq and Iran, consolidating its hold on the Caspian region and supporting Iraq and Iran's successful intimidation of the Gulf Co-operation Council – all in order to encourage high oil prices. The result is a less stable Middle East, which European politicians may think is not primarily a European problem. But it also means that Russia may eventually be able to set the price of oil, at least for the Europeans. Europeans would then have to go to Moscow to ask for relief, which they could get at a political price. Most likely this would take the form of future financial concessions".[14]

No one can deny that links between Russia and the European Union have intensified. Both partners are engaged in talks on plans to allow Russia to export its oil and gas to the European Union, where demand for energy is expected to rise sharply in the future. Continuing European investment in the Russian energy industry and pipelines has kept the ageing Soviet energy infrastructure from collapsing and has made Europe dependent on Russia. In the 1990's a parade of European companies entered into strategic alliances with Gazprom (Italy's ENI and Royal Dutch Shell). In the course of the year 2000, separate EU member states concluded bilateral treaties with Russia on the reconstruction of Russian pipeline systems in exchange for delivery of Russian natural gas to the Western partner. Russia now provides about half of Germany's hydrocarbons and roughly a third of Europe's as a whole. Direct dependence will grow in the next decade. Senior EU competition officials spoke out against the creation of a new breed of mega-firms in Russia, saying they would curb long-term economic efficiency and damage growth prospects. Alexander Schaub, European Commission Director General for Competition, put it like this: "Russia's young competition officials face the daunting task of introducing an element of healthy competition into monopolies like oil, gas, electricity production, transportation and telecommunications".[15]

5. A Triangular Relation: Russia-EU-US?

Russia's focus in its bid to regain the world's respect as a power to be reckoned with has shifted away from the United States and toward Europe since Putin came to power in 2000. Zbigniew Brzezinski declared that "the real goal must be to bring Russia into Euro-Atlantic security structures". But Germany does not want to provoke Russia by bringing the Baltic states into an enlarged NATO membership, while the US thinks that the Baltics need and deserve NATO membership ("if Russia wants to be part of an integrated Europe, it is making a big mistake in resisting the integration of others like the Baltic states"). Most European leaders reacted bewildered in July 2000, when then president Clinton, speaking in Aachen (Germany) suggested that the EU and NATO must leave the doors open for the eventual membership of Russia and Ukraine. And yet, Bush's National Security advisor, Condoleezza Rice, suggested in a White House Briefing in May 2001 that the Bush administration views the integration of Russia with the European Union as the long-term solution to the Russian problem.

The European Common Foreign and Defence Policy shows an enormous lack of creativity in dealing with Russia. Some might even wonder whether the EU really has a strategy towards Russia. It is undeniable, however, that there are enormous differences – and even incompatibilities – in strategic and commercial interests between the US and Europe.

The EU has no interest in an unlimited enlargement towards Central and Eastern Europe, and certainly not in Russian membership in the EU. Although the basic concept around which the EU is built remains a peace zone in Europe that is as large as possible and is open to the rest of the world, its immediate interests are focused on self-restriction in the process of enlargement. An overhasty enlargement procedure will weaken the European Union as an effective institution. One can go as far as to say that, if things could be re-arranged, it would be better to propose to the Eastern European countries that they first co-operate with one another within a regional framework in order to strengthen democracy and the market, thus paving the way for subsequent integration. The urge for EU membership has eliminated all other – perhaps more advisable – solutions. Would not, for example, a "Marshall plan" launched by the EU for separate regions with different aims have served as a better preparation for pan-European integration? The burden of taking up these new democracies will be too heavy for the European Union, still in search of its own identity. It would also be easier to talk to a "surrounded" Russia, because it would feel less threatened. Russia, as a countervailing power, was indeed excluded in an unacceptable manner.

Putin says that Russia is a European state with a European vocation. In the last months he has frequently mentioned eventual membership in NATO and the EU. The examples of German or Swedish democracy are models Putin wants Russia to follow. However, there are suspicions within the Bush administration that Putin is playing the old Soviet tactic of trying to play off Europe against the US. Therefore Bush's prime objective is to ensure that the transatlantic alliance holds firm and that Europe and the US agree to a common policy for dealing with Russia.

Both the EU and the US have a common interest in good relations with Russia, as Russia still has the power of nuclear devastation. Russia responded with remarkable calm to the announcement of George W. Bush on 1 May 2001 that he will go on with the National Missile Defence Initiative. Russia is no longer a clear enemy, as during the Cold War. But is it a friend?

The fact that Russia is not a NATO or EU member, and probably never will be, makes one think about new paradigms in these relations. In principle we Europeans are better placed than our Transatlantic partners to understand the fears of Russia. But we are not assertive enough. "We do not have to promote political and social models for the sake of transatlantic solidarity which no European leader would dare to impose on his own electorate".[16] As good Europeans, basing ourselves on Christian values, we should stand for social justice and a broad concept of peace. We should react against the increasing influence of a military industrial model (i.e. arms production and trade) and a military concept of European security.

All this illustrates that there is an urgent need for a new institutional and geopolitical concept of Europe. The post-war institutions and divisions cannot guarantee a future peace on the European continent, because they will divide Europe between the "Ins" and the "Outs", creating a new 'Schengen Curtain' or an economic or technological division in Europe. We need a strategic partnership, but not exactly in the way Russia sees it. We need a new partnership for peace, but not exactly in the way NATO wants it to develop. The European Union should define its own notion of "strategic partnership" and impose it on Russia as well as on the United States.

6. Strategic Partnership and European Security

Missile defence will figure prominently in US-EU debates. The overriding objective of any missile defence should be to defend the United States and its friends and allies against the "rogue state" missile threat; it should not be aimed at Russia, or China.

Russia and China have said they want to counter the weight of the US as the sole remaining power and have spoken almost as one in rejecting Washington's missile defence plans. Putin has sought to keep close ties with China, which he also considers as an important future economic partner, in particular as a customer for weapons.

It is equally clear that the future security of the European continent will depend on relations with Russia. The question is, what security (i.e. what concept of security) are we really talking about? Conflict prevention, peacekeeping and other elements of "soft security" have been a "trade mark" of European security for many years and it is preferable that this policy should be furthered in EU-Russian relations. Without a doubt, the creation of a stable security environment in Europe and the creation of a common security system is in the interest of the EU, but how will the EU avoid being drawn into one or the other "camp"? The core problem is that the European Union has not developed enough of its own political security identity in order to be able to interfere in conflicts within and outside the European Union.

Russia can certainly prove competence in structuring areas around itself. "It has become obvious that only Moscow is able to control 'hot-spots' and ensure stable access to natural deposits. Russia is able to avert such emergencies as the Taliban invasion and inter-state and inter-ethnic conflicts, and to eliminate international terrorism in CIS countries".[17] The question remains, however, how far Russia will go in structuring areas around itself: Will it establish a *cordon sanitaire*? Will it further regional co-operation along the line, for example, of its Union with Belarus?

The initiative to provide the European union with an 'operational crisis management staff' should strengthen the military capacity of the European Union and enable it to act in a more autonomous way. A European crisis intervention team of 60,000 people should be able to take peacekeeping measures and to organise small interventions in an independent way.[18] On December 4th, 2000, the European Council of Nice made a report on the preparedness of the member states to build a capacity in this field. At that stage Russia was asked again to participate in the EU-led operations.[19] It is clear that the Rapid Reaction Force of the European Union will only become a reliable instrument when NATO guarantees an effective intervention. But why is Russia excluded from a real partnership in this Rapid Reaction Force, as most conflicts situate themselves in Central and Eastern Europe? The Common Strategy towards Russia explicitly mentions the possibility of common initiatives in the field of conflict prevention, for example, in regions close to the Russian border or in the Near East. In the same text, the European Union declared its preparedness to see if and in which form co-operation with EU military crisis management operations can be organised or how common initiatives to strengthen the non-proliferation of weapons of mass destruction can be undertaken.

The long-term maximalist proposals of Russia are aimed at creating strong structures for European security policy, which will be able to counter NATO-centrism in Europe and to achieve long-term political-military co-operation with the European Union. Russia knows that neither the EU nor NATO will allow Russia to interfere in EU internal affairs. Co-operation will be restricted to information, consultations, and invitations to participate in EU initiatives on civil or military crisis management. In this sense, a Russian veto is excluded. Russia will probably be supported by a majority of member states when it proposes that an OSCE mandate for military crisis intervention will serve as a necessary condition for intervention, and this implies the co-operation of Russia.

From the Russian perspective, co-operation is attractive in those political fields where the European Union has some affinities with Russian interests, where the European Union takes a position clearly distinct from that of the United States or where EU-Russia co-operation can present itself as an alternative to co-operation with the US. This is the case, for example, in the Transcaucasian and Central Asian region. Moscow reproaches the US that they are pursuing their own national interests in this region and that their military presence in the region is aimed at achieving long-term influence in this territory which is rich in oil and gas. For Moscow, the alternative could be that the European Union as a political-economic actor with limited regional military capacity could become involved. This involvement of the European Union would leave more room for the protection of Russian 'vital interests' in the region. For example: Russia and some EU states see pipelines for Caspian oil through Iran as being more useful than the Ceyhan pipeline preferred by the US through Turkey and Georgia.[20]

7. The Role of "Zwischen-Europa" (Baltics and Central Europe)

The Central European countries are the first to react against any delay in accession and against any change of the profile of NATO as a defence organisation: NATO and the European Union are for them guarantees against Russian aggression. In a speech delivered on May 11th, 2001 at the Bratislava summit of NATO candidate countries, Vaclav Havel said that NATO must expand to include the entire geographic and culturally historic area commonly perceived as "the West" and that this area extends from Alaska in the West to Tallin in the East. He said this is a large territory but one that is comparable with the Russian Federation in terms of area and smaller in terms of population than the people's republic of China.[21]

Havel said that Russia's opposition to NATO stems both from the legacy of the Soviet era in which NATO used to be portrayed as an arch-enemy and from Russia's problem with its identity or self-understanding. He said Russia is still grappling with the problem that has marked its entire history, namely where its begins and where it ends; what belongs to its domain and what is beyond that domain where it should exercise decisive influence and from which point onward it can no longer do so. Havel says this reflects a lack of natural self-confidence, which comes to be expressed not only in the bombastic nationalism of characters such as Duma Deputy speaker and LDPR leader Zhirinovsky, but also in more cultured forms. It is absurd, according to the Czech president, that in the era of missiles a great nuclear power such as Russia should wish to build a 'cordon sanitaire' around itself.[22]

8. Conditions for a Strategic Partnership

A partner – and here we come back to the notion of strategic partnership – is someone one wants to work with in a transparent environment, with a clear aim, and in mutual interest. What will that environment be? A common European home? Pan-Europe? A new division of Europe between East and West – or Rome and Byzantium?

As EU enlargement will bring the EU's membership to Russia's doorstep, we should change our logic by thinking in a different way about a united Europe. The West still argues that Russia cannot claim the right to contribute to decision making in European institutions, such as the European Union and NATO, without being a member. This sounds logical, especially in view of Russia's attempt to influence the internal rules of the game. In this situation the creation of a greater Europe on the basis of western institutions may provoke a new European bipolarity.

The European Union should start from the clear assumption that Russia should be involved, but at the same time the European Union should be aware that a country like Russia will never be able or willing to integrate. It is unrealistic to hope for Russian integration into a Western European community of values in the short, medium or long term. The mistrust of Russia towards the West is linked to a weak feeling of national identity. This self-concept should be taken seriously and recognised by Western Europe as the cause of fundamental differences in national identity perception and foreign policy.

In this sense it would be preferable for the European Union to recognise, for the time being, that there are "several Europes". Instead of furthering the ideology of building a "common European House" or a "pan-European future", the European Union should focus on its own identity and its place in a larger Europe. This would imply that the European Union should take a differentiated attitude towards Central Europe, the Balkans, and the CIS. Even a Kaspian Stability Pact for avoiding Balkanisation of the region is conceivable within this framework of thought. To ensure a normal collaboration with Europe, Russia should be recognised as the leader of the CIS, defined as a relatively independent integration group within a multipolar world economic system. Russia's special path in the world should become the assumption of a policy towards the Balkan countries and Central Europe as regional blocs.

Within the geopolitical field of the CIS, the European Union should recognise Russian ambitions and be realistic about them. Moscow's interests are mainly economic and security oriented. The European Union is for Russia a major trade, transformation, and modernisation partner. The European Union cannot remain blind to the impact European enlargement will have on future economic and trade policy in Russia. The Kaliningrad "puzzle" can be considered in that perspective as a mythological presentation of the future confrontation of Russia with an enlarged Europe. Kaliningrad as a microcosm of Russian society illustrates that Russia has a stake in enlargement. On the other hand, the question of Kaliningrad illustrates the fact that the EU is contradicting its own principles by protecting its economy and closing its borders.[23]

That Russia should join – or in some way draw closer to – the European Union is perhaps hypothetically possible, but it is not realistic, since it would entail the inevitable limitation of national sovereignty owing to the transfer of a considerable portion of foreign and defence policy towards Brussels. It would be preferable to develop relations with a united Europe on the basis of the available comprehensive Partnership and Cooperation Agreement, which is largely based on the norms of the World Trade Organisation, so that the Russian industries can use it to the full. This would imply that the European Union should exclude the possibility that Russia will ever be accepted as a member of NATO or of the European Union. The thought of future Russian EU membership, which has been advanced by both sides (US and Russia), is dangerous for the European Union.

The problem of the Baltic countries, which are not included in the CIS framework but are clearly of major importance for Russian trade and security policy, makes it clear that the European Union cannot be blind to the implications of further NATO enlargement. Stabilisation measures are useless when NATO enlargement reaches to the Baltic states.

On the other hand, in addition to its identity as an economic power, the European Union should develop a strong security and foreign policy identity so that it can become a partner in political and security matters. Russia should be able to deal with the European Union as a player in the security field, and stop dealing with separate EU member states in these matters.[24]

The European Union should build another security structure with Russia other than NATO. NATO enlargement will spoil things for the European Union. Within this new security structure, Russia should be able to participate in the Rapid Reaction Force of the European Union. The success of enhanced co-operation in this field depends upon the question of whether European military crisis management will develop in the future towards an independent decision-making process with an autonomous capacity to activate this process. The question is whether EU states see such independence from NATO as useful and whether the US will not react negatively to this.

The European Union should further its 'structural' foreign policy objective of building stability through sustaining democracy and human rights protection. Building the infrastructure of an East-West traffic axis is equally part of this strategy. Confidence building measures are of key importance: training of the Russian elite on the level of jurisdiction, management, and social and economic policy. On the other hand, an uncontrolled development of capitalistic structures such as holdings and giant shareholder structures should be exposed as unhealthy for the development of a market economy and competition.

A reinvigorated policy is needed to prevent countries from acquiring missiles and weapons of mass destruction. In our research at universities we should in one way or another make more explicit that a military industrial model is a reprehensible way to guarantee European security. The European defence model contradicts the common interest of Europe and Russia, which is solidarity based on a concept of social justice and peace.

After having recognised each other's identity and having rejected the utopia of pan-Europe, the European Union and Russia can build a "partnership for peace" in co-ordinating their foreign policy in a constructive way towards the Near East, Islam, China, the UN and OSCE. This means that the focus should be on peace building measures, on the harmony of interests, on dialogue, and on co-ordinating the fight against international crime. This could increase the political weight of both powers in multilateral institutions such as the UN. In this sense, a strategic partnership could lead to a mutual interest in building world peace. World peace will in our view provide a better basis for the EU-Russian strategic partnership than the building of a "common European home".

Notes

1   One interesting source of information on the EU enlargement process is a separate weekly edition of Agence Europe: *Uniting Europe. The European Integration Bulletin for Central and Eastern Europe and the NIS.*

2   Mendelson S. "Democracy Assistance and Political Transition in Russia", *International Security,* Spring 2001, vol. 25 Issue 4, p. 68.

3   For an interesting overview of EU-Russia relations: "Inside (and beyond) Russia and the FSU", *Monthly Intelligence Bulletin of the European Press Agency,* vol. 9, no. 11- 22 November 2000. Special Issue: Russia and the European Union, 57p.

4   Council of the European Union: Common Strategy of the European Union towards Russia 04.06.1999: http://ue.eu.int/pesc/default.asp?lang=de

5   The EU-Russia Partnership and Cooperation Treaty was concluded in 1994: "Agreement on Partnership and Cooperation: establishing a partnership between the European Communities and their member states, and the Russian Federation": (http://www.fco.gov.uk/text_only/directory/expmemtxt.asp?/. The treaty came into force on 1 Dec 1997. The EU-Russia Cooperation Council, which convenes twice a year, has become an important instrument for EU-Russia policy. It finds its legal basis in the Partnership and Cooperation Treaty of 1994. The Cooperation Council first met on 27 January 1998 in Brussels: http://www.dgap.org/IP/ip9810/kom170198.htm

6 *Uniting Europe,* January 2001, no. 125.
7 The Medium Term Strategy for the Development of Relations between the Russian Federation and the European Union was presented as a document from the Ministry of Foreign Affairs and brought by President Putin to the EU summit of Helsinki in October 1999.
8 The chairman of the Foreign and Defense Policy Council is Sergei Alexandrovich Karaganov, the director of the Institute of Europe (*Institut Evropy*) of the Russian Academy of Sciences: http://www.svop.ru
9 See: Malfliet K. "The Commonwealth of Independent States: Russia's Ambitions disguised in a European (Eurasian) Project?", in: Tom Casier and Katlijn Malfliet (Eds.), *Is Russia a European Power? The Position of Russia in a New Europe,* Leuven University Press, 1998, 91-129.
10 "Inside (and beyond) Russia and the Former Soviet Union", o.c., note 3, p.4.
11 Timmerman H. "Russlands Strategie für die Europäische Union", in: *Berichte des Bundesinstituts für ostwissenschaftliche und internationale Studien,* 5-2000.
12 Conclusions of the EU-Russia summit (Paris 30 October 2000): http://www.doc.diplomatie.fr./cgi-bin/go_doc.pl?type=bull&cible= 20001102.1.de.html#chapitre2
13 "Inside (and beyond) Russia and the Former Soviet Union", o.c., note 3, p.9.
14 Angelo Codevilla (professor of international relations at Boston University), "Europe's Dangerous Alliance with the Bear", *Wall Street Journal Europe,* 7 June 2001.
15 *Johnson's Russia List,* 26 April 2001, 15.
16 "Inside (and beyond) Russia and the former Soviet Union", o.c., note 3, p.8.
17 Tarasov S. "The World after the Cold War. Will a new Security Cordon be Established around Russia?", *Vek,* no. 46 (translated by Ria Novosti).
18 The heads of governments at the EU summits in Köln (June 1999), Helsinki (December 1999) and Feira (June 2000) decided that up to 2001 the EU member states should be able to delegate 5000 men for international missions and they should be able to settle conflicts within 30 days in crisis regions: http://ue.eu.int/pesc/default.asp?lang=en
19 Ibidem.
20 Bernhof I. "Europa und Russland – Zwischenbilanz und Ausblick", Berlin Information Center for Transatlantic Security (BITS), http://www.bits.de/ public/briefingnote/bn01-1.htm
21 *RFE/RL Newsline,* vol.5, n°91, part II, 14 May 2001.
22 Ibidem.
23 Conference: The Northern Dimension and the Kaliningrad region, 17-18 May 2000, Copenhagen, http://www.um.dk/udenrigspolitik/oesteuropa/sng/ konference
24 Bernhof, o.c., note 14.

LIST OF CONTRIBUTORS

Katlijn Malfliet (°1954) studied Law and Philosophy at the Catholic University of Leuven. After obtaining a MA in Eastern European Studies (RUG-KUL-VUB), she wrote her doctoral thesis on Property Law in the Soviet Union among others at the Academy of Sciences in Moscow. She studied Russian in Leuven, Brussels and Moscow. As visiting professor she taught at the universities of Leiden, Moscow and Prague. At the Catholic University of Leuven, she teaches courses on political, social and juridical transition in Central and Eastern Europe.

As research director for Central and Eastern Europe of the Institute for International and European Policy, Katlijn Malfliet leads several research and development projects about transition in the post-communist countries (mainly the Russian Federation). The main research topics are: privatisation and institutional reform and the link between culture, politics and law. Professor Malfliet wrote several books on these topics: *De moeilijke weg naar democratie en markt in Midden-en Oost-Europa* (Davidsfonds, 1993) ; *Intellectual Property Rights in Russia: A System in Transition* (Bruylant, 1994) ; *Alternatieven voor het teloorgegane communisme* (ed), (Garant, 1994) ; *Regionalism in Russia* (IEB, 1995) ; *Towards the Rule of Law in Russia* (IEB, 1996) ; *Wie is bang voor Oost-Europa ?* (ed.), (Garant, 1997) *; Minority Policy in Central and Eastern Europe* (co-edited with R. Laenen, Garant, 1998) ; (co-edited with T. Casier) *Is Russia a European Power ? The Position of Russia in a New Europe.* (Universitaire Pers Leuven, 1999) ; *Het Europees Beleid van Rusland* (co-edited with L. Verpoest, Garant, 2000).

Margot Light is Professor of International Relations at the London School of Economics and Political Science. She is co-author (with Neil Malcolm, Alex Pravda and Roy Allison) of *Internal Factors in Russian Foreign Policy* (1996) and co-editor (with Karen Smith) of *Ethics and Foreign Policy* (2001). Her most recent articles are (with Stephen White and John Löwenhardt) 'A Wider Europe: The View from Moscow and Kyiv', *International Affairs* 76:1 (January 2000) and 'Russian Perspectives on European Security' in *European Foreign Affairs Review*, 5:4 (2000), "You no longer believe in us and we no longer believe in you": Russian attitudes towards Europe', in Helen Wallace, ed., Interlocking Dimensions of European Integration. Palgrave, 2001, 'Belorussiya, Moldaviya, Ukraina: k vostoku ili k zapadu?' (Belarus, Moldova and Ukraine: eastward or westward looking?') [in Russian], Mirovaya ekonomika i mezhdunarodnye otnosheniya, No. 7 (2001); and (with John Löwenhardt and Ronald Hill) 'A wider Europe: the view from Minsk and Chisinau', International Affairs 77:3 (2001).

Konstantin K. Khudoley (°1951) obtained the degree of Doctor of Science at the Faculty of History at Saint Petersburg State University in 1988. Professor of History until 1991. From 1991 until 1994, Professor and Head of Department at the Faculty of Political Science. Since 1994 Dean of the Faculty of International Relations. His research topics are Russian foreign policy and the relations between Russia and the West. Professor Khudolej has more than 50 publications on International Relations, politics and history of Europe. He became Doctor Honoris Causa at International Marychrist University, USA in 1999. Furthermore, he was Saint Petersburg city councillor from 1990 – 1993, and is expert to various Government and Public Organisations. Professor Khudolej is also Member of the Association of European Studies, the Russian Association of International Studies, the Academy of Political Science, the Academy of Humanity (Russia), the Association Of International Studies (USA), the Central and East European International Studies Association (1996 – 1999 President of CEEISA)

Yuri A. Borko (°1929) Doctor in Economic Sciences, Professor, Head of the Centre for European Integration Studies and Jean Monnet Chair for European Integration Studies, Institute of Europe, Russian Academy of Sciences. Professor Borko graduated from Moscow University, Faculty of History in 1953. He worked as a Junior Researcher at the Institute of World Economy and International Relations in 1962-63. He was editor and executive secretary of the Journal "The World Economy and International Relations" (1963-70). He was Head of Department at the Institute of Information on Social Sciences from 1970 until 1989. Previous positions at the Institute of Europe – Head of Department (1990-95), Deputy Director (1995-98).
Author of several books and a great number of articles on various aspects of European integration, the EEC/EU activities and Russia-EU relations published in the USSR/Russia and abroad. President of Association of European Studies (Russia) from 1992, when this scientific non-governmental organisation was established.

Jan Kerkhofs (°1924) Member of the Society of Jesus. Studied in Leuven, Oxford, Münster. Former professor of sociology (University of Antwerp), of moral theology (Jesuit Faculty), emeritus professor of the Faculty of Theology, Catholic University of Leuven. Doctor Honoris Causa University Tilburg. Former secretary-general of the international Foundation *'Pro Mundi Vita'*, Brussels. Founder of the Foundation *European Values Study*. Chairman of the Cardinal Alfrink Peace Fund. Honorary member of the Foundation *Arval* (values research), Paris. Member of the *Interfaith Foundation*, London. Vice-President of *Cafe*, Cambridge (U.K.). Former (1965-1995) spiritual adviser of *Uniapac* (international organisation for Christian business executives). Visiting professor in many universities. Author of more than 30 books and about 500 articles.

John Löwenhardt is Alexander Nove Professor of Russian and East European Studies and Director of the Institute of Central and East European Studies at the University of Glasgow (Scotland, UK). Previously he was at the Universities of Amsterdam and Leiden (The Netherlands). In 1995 he published *The Reincarnation of Russia: Struggling with the Legacy of Communism, 1990-1994.* (Durham N.C., Duke University Press), in 1998 he edited the volume on *Party Politics in Post–Communist Russia* and in 2001 (with David Betz) *Army and State in Postcommunist Europe* (both: London & Portland, Frank Cass). With Margot Light and Stephen White he is currently involved in an ESRC funded research project on the impact of NATO and EU-expansion on the 'outsider-states' Russia, Ukraine, Belarus and Moldova.

Lien Verpoest (°1977), Master in Eastern European Languages and Culture (1995-1999). She studied at the K.U. Leuven, in Russia (Saint Petersburg State University) and Sweden (University of Lund). She wrote her Master's Thesis about conservative tendencies in 19th century Russia. Lien Verpoest also holds a post-graduate degree in International Relations and Conflict Management (2000). For this degree, she wrote a Master's Thesis on the Eastward Enlargement of the European Union. In 2001, she obtained an M.A. in Eastern European Studies. In the framework of the Chair Interbrew-Baillet Latour on the Relations between Russia and the European Union, she conducts research on institutional and geo-political changes in the relations between Russia and Europe. Other research topics also include Russian foreign policy and the relations within between the three countries of the Slavic Core of the CIS: Russia, Belarus and Ukraine.

Dmitry A. Danilov (°1960), graduated from Moscow University, economic department in 1982, from where he obtained his Ph.D. (economics) in 1987. He works as the Head of the Department for European Security Studies in the Institute of Europe, Moscow, Russian Academy of Sciences. Previously (1982-1989), he worked as a senior researcher in the analytic cell of the General Staff. Dmitry Danilov is author of more than 70 scientific publications. Took part in preparation of analytical reports for state and governmental bodies of Russia and for international organisations, including NATO. Specialises in problems of European security institutions, military-political aspects of the transatlantic relationship, Russian security policy; also published some works on peace-keeping and conflict prevention as well as defence economics. Dr. Danilov headed the Russian side of the common research project undertaken in 1996-1998, following ministerial indications, by the Institute for Security Studies of the Western European Union and Institute of Europe of the Russian Academy of Sciences with the purpose of finding the ways and modalities for enhanced relationship between the RF and WEU/EU in the security field.

Vladimir Ronin (°1958) holds a Ph.D. in History and an MA in Slavic Philology. He studied history at the University of Moscow and Slavic Philology at the Catholic University of Leuven. Since 1990, he works in Belgium and teaches Russian and Russian Studies at Lessius Hogeschool Antwerpen. Dr. Ronin is the author of a.o. *Antwerpen en zijn 'Russen', 1814-1914* (1993; de Russian version 1994); *Russen en Belgen: is het water te diep?* (1998); *Regiony Rossii* (1996, 1999); *Zdravstvujte, Mister Najf!* (1999) and *Media i millennium.* He is co-author of *Het land van de Blauwe Vogel. Russen in België* (1991) and also writes about Medieval History of Central and Eastern Europe and the relations between Belgium and Russia throughout the centuries.

Ioann Ekonomtsev (°1939) is the Rector of the University of St. John the Divine (Ioann Bogoslov) in Moscow and Chairman of Department for Religious Education and Catechism of the Moscow Patriarchate for all Russia. He graduated from the Msocow State University, Philology Department. Later, he was employed by the Ministry of Culture and the Ministry of Foreign Affairs. He worked in Greece at the Russian Embassy and at the Academy of Sciences. He started giving lectures at the Moscow Spiritual Academy since 1983. He has been a deacon and priest since 1986.

Koen Vanheusden (°1962) works since 1986 as juridical advisor at the Belgian Foreign Trade Service. There, he helps exporters to find practical answers to judicial and regulatory questions concerning their trade with and in Europe, Central and Eastern Europe, including the Russian Federation and the CIS countries. Mr. Vanheusden also participated in several commissions about the trade between Belgium and the Russian Federation. He has also written several articles and given lectures about this topic, among others in the framework of the EMBA Moscow and the MTP-programme of TACIS.